Deer Camp Devotions

A Season of 30 Devotions for the Month of November

Rev. Dr. Roland C. Lindeman

DEER CAMP DEVOTIONS

Copyright © 2012 Roland C. Lindeman

All rights reserved.

ISBN: 9781075032608

DEDICATION

I am dedicating this book to the two patriarchs of the deer camps where I have hunted for so many years, Elmer and Kenneth and to their respective sons who have welcomed me into their camps so graciously, Roger and Jerry.

DEER CAMP DEVOTIONS

CONTENTS

	Acknowledgments	i
1	Trust the Compass!	1
2	First deer I ever shot.	4
3	Too close for comfort.	6
4	Feeling used and abused.	8
5	Lighting a fire in my blind.	10
6	Lucky shot / Unlucky deer.	12
7	Lighting another fire.	15
8	Big Buck Story part 1.	17
9	Big Buck Story part 2.	20
10	Buck Slayer	22
11	Bringing the trophy home.	24
12	A Sticky Situation.	26
13	The Buck Alarm	28
14	Lighting yet another fire!	30
15	The Buck that got away.	33
16	A Nice Buck for a Good Friend.	36
17	The Buck that wasn't a Buck.	39
18	Building a new blind.	42
19	"Mr. Spikey!"	44
20	Switching Ammunition.	46

21	Locked in a blind.	48
22	There are Bear in the woods.	50
23	Surrounded by Turkeys.	52
24	Remembering Dear Hunting Friends	55
25	Drinking coffee in a tree stand.	57
26	"Bonnie's Buns" and other deer camp delicacies.	59
27	Leaving the blind too early.	61
28	An eight point spike!	63
29	How dark is the swamp?	66
30	What happens at Camp stays at Camp!	69

DEER CAMP DEVOTIONS

ACKNOWLEDGMENTS

I am extremely grateful for the encouragement of my deer hunting family in Michigan, for the encouragement of my own family and for the support of my current congregation, Emmanuel Lutheran Church in Seymour, WI who gave me enough time away on a recent sabbatical in order to work on this project.

TRUST THE COMPASS!

I never really had a chance to go deer hunting until I graduated from Seminary and accepted my first call to a congregation in Northern Minnesota located on the "Iron Range." "There's a lot of good deer hunting around here," a member of the congregation told me," and so I began shopping for a hunting rifle. I was just out of school and our son, Tony was only 4 years old, so money was tight. Still, I watched the classified ads and came across a listing for a "deer rifle for sale: WWII Japanese, re-bored to 30-06, $50." I went out to look at the rifle, knowing pretty much nothing about it, and decided to go ahead and purchase my first deer rifle. That November, I was ready to go deer hunting. Except for the fact that I had no idea where I would go. I asked around and was told that public hunting was allowed in the Superior National Forest, which was not that far away from where we lived. I took a trip one day, before season, to check it out. I found a place about 100 yards into the forest, that looked like it might be a good hunting location, so I marked the spot with a red ribbon on a tree alongside of the road where I had walked in.

I wasn't able to go on the opening day of season, but I managed to take some time in the middle of the first week of hunting to head out to that spot. I got up before dawn and drove to the place where I had tied the ribbon. It was still there! I checked my compass before heading into the woods so that I would know which direction I needed to go in order to get back to my car. It was a very cold morning in Northern Minnesota.

I didn't know for sure how cold until later that day when I heard that the temperature at the time I walked into the woods was -42 degrees! I walked for some distance into the woods and found a place to sit on a stump and I sat there and waited. I waited for what seemed like a long time, looking at the heavy snow hanging from the trees and listening for any sounds that might indicate a deer was moving. Finally, I couldn't sit any longer. I decided to get up and move around. That's when I saw some fresh tracks in the snow. "All right," I thought, "a deer has walked through here recently." I decided to follow the tracks. I'm not sure how long or how far I followed those tracks but I know that at some point I stopped and looked around and realized I had no idea where I was. I checked my compass to see which direction I needed to go to get back to the road where my car was parked. According to the compass, I needed to head in the exact opposite direction from where I was thinking I should go. "That can't be right," I remember thinking to myself, "This compass must not be working."

I almost started walking away from where the compass indicated I should go when a small airplane flew overhead. It was coming in for a landing at a local airport that was near where I had parked my car. When I saw the direction the plane was heading I realized that the compass was correct. So, I turned around and followed the compass, finally, to the road. I came out on the road about ½ mile from where my car was parked. In telling this story to members of the congregation I found out that if I had kept heading East instead of West, I would have probably never been found. "The Superior National Forest goes for over 100 miles in that direction," they told me. "Good thing that plane came over at just the right time!" Good thing indeed!

Now I know that some people would want to say that God was watching over me on that day and that somehow God made sure that plane was flying overhead when it did.

While I am thankful that plane did fly overhead, I am pretty sure it was just dumb luck. I do believe, however, that God was with me. He was and is always with me, reminding me to be His Child and to be led by His Holy Spirit.

In a way, the Holy Spirit is like a compass. As a compass always points North so that you can determine which direction is the right direction to travel, God's Holy Spirit is always pointing us to the cross, so that we might know how much God loves us and gave himself up for us and how it is also that He calls us to love other people and give ourselves up for the sake of others.

Just because a compass points us in the right direction, doesn't mean that we will always go in that direction. We can, and sometimes do, choose to ignore the compass.

In the same way that we can, and often do, choose to be unloving and self-serving. Still God is with us. He never stops loving us even when we go the wrong direction and make the wrong choices. He sticks with us and promises that there is nothing that can separate us from His love.

"What then are we to say about these things? If God is for us, who is against us? ³²He who did not withhold his own Son, but gave him up for all of us, will he not with him also give us everything else? -- ³⁷No, in all these things we are more than conquerors through him who loved us. ³⁸For I am convinced that neither death, nor life, nor angels, nor rulers, nor things present, nor things to come, nor powers, ³⁹nor height, nor depth, nor anything else in all creation, will be able to separate us from the love of God in Christ Jesus our Lord." (Romans 8:31, 32; 3-39)

PRAYER: Faithful God, as I consider the many bad decisions and poor choices that I have made in my life, I am grateful for the promise that you have given that in all "these things," there is still nothing that can separate us from your love. Continue to guide me by your Spirit even as you walk with me each step of the way. Amen.

THE FIRST DEER I EVER SHOT

It was the middle of August and I was still considered a new comer to the U.P. having just recently moved from northern Minnesota, when I received a phone call from one of the members of my new congregation. Edgar had heard that I was interested in deer hunting and so he was calling to see if I would like to come over to his farm and shoot a deer. "It's August," I replied, "I don't think it's legal to shoot a deer in August!" "Don't worry," Edgar responded, "I have plenty of crop damage permits so as long as you shoot a deer on my property it's perfectly legal." "Well ok then," I said, "I'll be right over!"

My son, Tony, was only 8 years old, but when he heard that I was going to shoot a deer, he wanted to come along. Tony and I showed up at Edgar's farm and he told us where to go to find the deer. "Follow this road to the stone fence and then take a left turn following the stone fence until you come to a bunch of junked cars and farm machinery. Be quiet as you turn the corner to the right around that pile of junk because that's where you find the deer grazing in a field."

We followed his instructions exactly as he had said, and sure enough, right around the corner past those junk cars there must have been over a hundred deer standing there, grazing in this small field of rye grass.

I was so surprised and amazed that I didn't really know what to do, I just stood there for a while looking at the deer, when my son said, "Dad, aren't you going to shoot one of them?" And I said, "Yes, Tony, I'm going to shoot one of them." So I lifted up my rifle and aimed through the scope trying to decide which one of them I would shoot. Edgar had told me that I couldn't shoot a buck, but only a doe so I picked out the biggest doe that was relatively close to where we were. I took aim and pulled the trigger and in an instant there was a loud noise and a hundred deer running into the woods, leaving only one deer left, lying on the ground. "You got him!" Tony shouted, and sure enough, I had killed my first deer.

Tony and I stood there looking over that deer that was lying in the field for some time and finally I took out my brand new "buck knife" and knelt down next to the deer to begin the process of field dressing. The only problem is I had no idea what to do or where to start. Tony realized that I was having problems and so he said, "Do you want me to go and get farmer Edgar?" And I said, "Sure, Tony that's a good idea!" And so, Tony ran off to get Farmer Edgar, and I made a feeble attempt to at least begin the process. Eventually, Edgar showed up riding his tractor and pulling a wagon with Tony riding right next to him. He helped me finish the job of dressing the deer and together we put it on the trailer in order to haul it back to my car. After loading the deer into the trunk of my car, Edgar turned to Tony and said, "Tony, I have a heifer that's freshening, how would you like to help me deliver a calf?" "Really?" Tony responded, "Sure!"

And so it was that on the same day that I shot my first deer, my son was able to witness the birth of a new calf. It was pretty amazing, the "circle of life" unfolding right before his young eyes.

My son is now over 40 years old, but we still talk about that day and about that experience. Birth and Death are the bookends of our life. More important than shooting a deer, even my first deer, was being able to share this moment with my son and being able to talk with him about such things as birth and death within the context of faith in God.

The undeniable realities of birth and death could cause a person to assume a kind of fatalistic attitude about such things. Perhaps one might be tempted to think that there are limited benefits to being born and facing the challenges and struggles of each day. Still, when the reality of death is experienced in parallel with the amazing miracle of birth, a manger, a cross and an empty tomb, it is possible to celebrate both birth and death, trusting in God's resurrection promise.

[24]*Very truly, I tell you, unless a grain of wheat falls into the earth and dies, it remains just a single grain; but if it dies, it bears much fruit. (John 12)*

I am glad to say that Tony recently shot his first deer. He has also experienced the miracle of birth with the gift of our first grandchild. God is good and His promise is certain; each day that we live with all of its challenges and struggles is a gift to celebrate as we hope for the greatest gift of all, eternal life.

PRAYER: Loving God, let me never take the gift of each day for granted. May the promise of your eternal love allow me to celebrate both birth and death always within the context of Faith, Hope and Love. AMEN.

DEER CAMP DEVOTIONS

TOO CLOSE FOR COMFORT

One of the very first times I was privileged to hunt with a group of hunters with whom I have now been hunting for over 25 years I was both excited and nervous about the opportunity to join the group on a deer hunting "drive." The idea behind a "drive" is that there are several hunters who walk through a swamp, hoping to drive out any deer that may be lying down in the thick brush. While those "drivers" or "dogs" as they are sometimes called are walking through the swamp there are several other hunters that are stationed at strategic locations waiting to shoot any buck that may be spooked out of its hiding and make a run for safety out of the swamp. I was told that my job on that day would be to be one of the hunters posting on an edge of the swamp. "Be ready," my experienced friend told me, "because where you are standing is a 'hot spot' where very often deer that are spooked will run out. "Be ready," he said, "you won't have much time when a deer comes." And then he pointed to a trail coming out of the swamp where I might expect to see a deer running out. "Be ready!"

I was ready. Or, at least I thought I was ready. I stood there on alert waiting for something to happen but as time went by and nothing seemed to be happening, I began to wonder and my mind started wandering as I thought about these strange surroundings that stood before me. It was a cold November day and snow was on the ground, I was standing on an old logging road with a swamp in front of me and a large corn field behind me. As I looked into the swamp, it was hard to see anything or even hear any noise. It seemed strangely quiet. As I looked across the corn field, I was thinking how different this corn field looked compared to the corn fields that I was used to seeing in Nebraska where I grew up. The corn fields in Nebraska are flat and lay out in forty acre sections. This corn field in the Upper Peninsula of Michigan had rolling hills and sharp angles. I began to wonder how in the world the farmer managed to plant and then cut the corn in this kind of terrain.

And then it happened. I heard someone in the swamp yell, "coming your way!" I heard a shot and the noise of branches breaking and before I had a chance to do more than just turn and look, there was a buck charging out of the swamp heading right at me. I had to jump just to get out of its way as it ran past me and out into the corn field, by the time I turned and raised my rifle it was already in the field and running at full speed.

I tried to get a line on it with my scope but I had never tried to shoot anything on the run before and never did even get off even a single shot. The deer was gone and my friend was coming out of the woods wondering, "what happened?" "Why didn't you shoot?"

"I don't know," I said, "I thought I was ready. It almost ran me over!"

Are you ready? "Carpe Deim," Robin Williams says to the students in his class in the movie, "The Dead Poets Society." Seize the day, don't hesitate, be ready because even when you think you're ready, the challenges of life sometimes come charging at you so fast that all you have time to do is try and just get out of the way.

The good news is that even though I failed at this first attempt of hunting with my friends from the U.P., they didn't give up on me. I took some good natured ribbing about how I managed to not shoot a deer when there was "deer hair on the end of my rifle barrel," and we are all still able to laugh about the experience. I have also learned from this experience to expect the unexpected. If it's true in deer hunting it is also true in life.

The good news is that God never gives up on us in life either. He calls us to be ready, to seize the day and not to hesitate when it comes to bearing witness to his love in this world where it so easy to be distracted by other things.

An angry parishioner, a thoughtless neighbor, an irrational relative can sometimes seem like they are charging right at us and all we want to do is just get out of their way. Be ready, don't hesitate, pull the trigger of God's love, grace and mercy and see what happens. Who knows, you might bag another "dear friend." Either way there is no doubt, that God will always be your best dear friend!

PRAYER: Loving God, keep me mindful of the importance of each moment in life as an opportunity to bear witness to your love. When distractions and temptations arise may your Holy Spirit call me again and again to be ready. When I falter and fail, remind me that you will never falter in your love and patience for me. AMEN.

FEELING USED AND ABUSED

It was another cold and snowy day in November. We were sitting around the table at camp playing cards when someone came up with the idea that this would be a good day to "drive Renner's swamp." The rationale was that on a day like this the big bucks would certainly be laying in the swamp trying to avoid exposure to the weather. One of the things that I have learned is that, at deer camp, just about any idea can at any moment seem like a really good idea. And so, off we went to drive "Renner's swamp."

My last experience on a deer drive was not very successful and so I was not all that sure that this really was a good idea, still, who am I to question the wisdom of those who have been doing such things for so long. So off we went. Once again it was determined that I should be one of those hunters who would be strategically placed on the outside of the swamp. Only this time, I was told that I should stand on the north side of the swamp, under a tree that stood right alongside of a county road. There was about twenty acres of a corn field that stood between where I was standing and where the swamp began. I was told that if I happened to shoot a deer and it ran into the neighboring field, just west of where I was standing, it would be no problem because I was the "pastor" and the person who owned that neighboring field would be less likely to be upset with me.

As the rest of the crew took up their positions around the swamp and the "drivers" or "dogs" began to make their way into the swamp, I suddenly realized that the drivers were walking into the swamp right in front of me and were heading south, into the swamp. I couldn't help but wonder, "What chance do I have at shooting a deer when they are driving the deer away from me?" That, together with the realization that I was also standing out in the open in the cold wind and blowing snow, made me begin to think that I was being "used and abused."

But then, just when I was about to give up, a deer came running out of the swamp heading directly toward where I was standing. I could see right away that it had horns. Without hesitating, I immediately raised my rifle and began shooting.

In retrospect, I did so without thinking either, because the buck was running toward me, I should have waited for it to get closer. Nevertheless,

I fired off five shots and the buck never even flinched. It did, however, change directions and began running toward the neighbor's field. I got down on my knees, pulled out my second clip and reloaded my rifle and fired off three more shots. Finally the buck tumbled to the ground, just before crossing the fence line into the neighbor's property.

I can't tell you how relieved I was to see that deer fall to the ground. As I came walking up to where the deer was laying, one of the other hunters who was posting on the east side of the swamp also came walking up. He had witnessed the whole thing and he said, "Pastor, when I saw you get down on your knees I thought you praying, but it turns out you were only reloading!" He then congratulated me on shooting my first buck and graciously field dressed the deer for me. Later on at camp, when we weighed the deer, they discovered that I had actually hit the deer with 5 of my eight shots. "No wonder it weighs so much," someone said, "it has 20 lbs. of lead in it!" So it goes at deer camp.

I learned some important lessons that day;
1. When a deer is running towards you, you don't have to start shooting right away!
2. When friends, who have been hunting for a long time, tell you where to stand, they are probably not trying to take advantage of you.
3. Even when a deer is hit, it may not fall to ground immediately.

In the unpredictable circumstances of life, these lessons are also important. Patience, Confidence and Trust are qualities that can lead to genuine success when we apply them to the relationships that we have with family, friends and with God.

If we patiently wait for the right opportunities to present themselves and then take our best shot at being the loving and caring person that we know God wants us to be, we can also trust that God will work through our best efforts to accomplish his will. The results of our efforts may not be immediately apparent, but we can still get down on our knees to pray even as Jesus did, when he prayed: "Father, not my will but your will be done!"

PRAYER: Gracious God, increase in me this day the gifts of patience, confidence and trust in the relationships that I have with other people and especially in the relationship that I am privileged to have with you through Jesus Christ. Amen.

LIGHTING A WOOD FIRE IN MY BLIND

I have hunted long enough to remember when the weather in November seemed to always be very cold with snow on the ground. Because there were no portable "propane" heaters available in those days, it wasn't uncommon for hunters to make their own, small wood stove heaters using whatever materials they had on hand.

This was exactly the case for the small deer blind that I was invited to use when I first started hunting with good friends in the U.P. of Michigan. Elmer, who was the patriarch of the family with whom I was hunting had taken a small 5 gallon empty oil can together with an old rain gutter and turned them into a miniature wood stove and chimney.

When I crawled into that deer blind before light on the first day of hunting season, I noticed that Elmer had not only provided this "home-made" wood stove, but that he had also provided a supply of wood, cut small enough to fit in the stove together with some kindling, newspaper and matches. For me, this was a wonderful and genuine example of U.P. hospitality.

That morning was not as cold as other mornings that I had already experienced on the opening day of deer season, but it was cold enough for me to be tempted by the prospect of a warm fire burning in that amazing little stove. As I recall, it didn't take very long before I set my rifle down and began the process of building a fire.

This was a very small deer blind so there wasn't a lot of room for me to be moving around. I had to get down on my knees in order to open up the stove and load it with paper, kindling and wood before striking a match and light the fire. Everything went very well, and as I was still on my knees I was already enjoying the warmth of the fire burning inside.

Once I knew that the fire was burning sufficiently, I lifted up my head to look out the window of my blind only to see that there was a 6 point buck standing directly in front of my blind, "standing" only about 10 feet away! I was on my knees with my rifle leaning against one of the corners behind me in the blind and that 6 point buck was just standing there, looking at the blind.

I lowered my head and began the slow process of quietly turning, reaching for my rifle, rising to a position from which I could actually get my rifle barrel pointed out of the window in order to take a shot, only to realize, when I lifted my head again, that this beautiful 6 point buck was not where in sight.

It was gone! I was warm, but I was experiencing, once again, that terrible feeling that you get when you know that you have just messed up and missed a great opportunity. This was not the first nor the last time that I would experience this disappointing feeling, but I have discovered in these situations that, having "been there before" doesn't ever seem to make it any easier.

I am reminded of words spoken by the Apostle Paul when he says;

"For I do not do the good I want to do, but the evil I do not want to do – this I keep on doing…..wretched man that I am! Who will rescue me from this body of death? Thanks be to God, through Jesus Christ our Lord!"(Romans 7: 15 – 25)

Whenever a person chooses to do what they do out of a desire to fulfill their own personal need for comfort and pleasure they may discover that in the end they can miss out on an opportunity to accomplish something even more important.

There is nothing more important than accomplishing the work that God gives us to do as witnesses in this world to His love. Sacrificing personal comfort or giving up some personal pleasure in order to provide such a witness can very often lead to a greater good, even greater than shooting a six point buck!

PRAYER: Gracious God, grant me the wisdom I need each day to see opportunities for doing the work of Your Kingdom and then the fortitude that I need to actually do it. Amen.

LUCKY SHOT, UNLUCKY DEER

After sitting all day for a couple of days at the beginning of the gun deer season, I had yet to see anything more than just a few squirrels and a couple of blue jays that kept flying back and forth across the power line opening that I was watching.

It wouldn't have been so bad except for the fact that the other hunters were all seeing lots of deer at their deer blinds and a couple of them had already bagged nice bucks, now hanging on the buck pole. So there I was on my last day of hunting, still watching squirrels and blue jays. I have to admit that I was starting to feel sorry for myself, "why am I so unlucky," I thought.

I was happy for the other hunters who had already shot nice bucks, but truth be told, I was also jealous and pretty disappointed. And then it happened. I saw a doe come running out of the woods into the power line opening that I was watching and right behind the doe was a buck. By the time that I got my rifle up and ready to shot, both deer had ducked back into the hard woods in front of me.

I could still see them running and so I picked out an opening between trees just behind where the doe was running and when I saw the buck entering into that opening, I fired a shot….and just like that, "bam!" the buck was laying on the ground. I dropped him right on the spot! Now I have to admit that I was feeling pretty darn good about myself, "wow, I am a good shot," I thought.

I got out of my blind and started to walk towards the deer, feeling pretty confident that it would be dead by the time I got there, only to discover that when I was about 20 yards away, suddenly that buck lifted up its head. It was still on the ground but its head was now straight up and it was looking at me!

I got down on one knee, took aim at its neck and fired another shot. Only now, the buck didn't even flinch. He was still just looking at me as if nothing had happened. I walked closer, now about 10 yards away, got down on one knee and took another shot at its neck. Still, the buck didn't even flinch. I couldn't believe it.

How could I miss at such close range? And yet, the buck was still just lying on the ground with its head straight up, looking at me. So, I walked slowly within 5 feet and I aimed at its neck and fired a shot and finally, that did it, the buck dropped its head and was soon dead. As a sighed a sigh of relief, I walked over to begin the field dressing process when I noticed something really odd about this buck.

On one of its rear hoofs there was a metal thermos ring, the top to a coffee thermos which this buck had evidently stepped into long enough ago that its hoof had grown too big for the metal thermos ring to come off. When he walked he would make three regular hoof prints and one circle print! I later found out that my rifle was not sighted in correctly; it was shooting about 12" high!

The first shot that I fired dropped the buck, only because I was shooting so high that the bullet broke the buck's back. That's why it couldn't move but was still very much alive. As it turns out, I was one lucky hunter and this was one "unlucky" buck! The truth is that while it takes a certain amount of skill and experience to bag a buck….. It also takes a little bit of luck, and sometimes even, a whole lot of luck!

We live in a world in which a lot of things are unpredictable. Things happen that are beyond our control, things that are both improbable and unimaginable. Sometimes these things work to our advantage and sometimes they work to our disadvantage.

Where is God in all of this? Some people who might want to say that when things go well God is blessing us and that when things do not go well, God is punishing us.

If that were the case then there would be no such thing as "luck." Everything that happens would be according to God's specific will to either bless or punish. I do not believe that this is the kind of God that Jesus reveals to us when He says, *"For this is the will of my Father, that everyone who looks on the Son and believes in him should have eternal life, and I will raise him up on the last day!" (John 6:40)*

Someone has suggested that "luck is the residue of good preparation." There may be a certain amount of truth to that. Had I sighted my rifle in better before the season started, I might have had a better experience on this particular day. However, it also true that no matter how well prepared you may be, a certain amount of uncertainty, to be lucky or unlucky, still exists.

God's promise is not that he will bless us with luck, or punish us with no luck. God's promise is that He will love us no matter what happens in our lives. His Grace and Mercy are dependent upon luck or even upon good preparation on our part. On the contrary, God's grace & mercy are sure and certain because they depend only upon Hiss good and gracious will and His unconditional love that has been poured upon us through Jesus Christ.

PRAYER: God of grace and mercy, give me each day the strength and courage that I need to face the uncertainties and disappointments of life with confidence knowing that your will is certain and sure and that you have promised to bless me not with "luck" but with love that is unconditional and eternal. AMEN.

LIGHTING ANOTHER FIRE....SMOKED OUT

You would think that after missing a nice 6 point buck because I was too busy lighting a fire in the little wood stove in my blind that I would be reluctant to try and light another fire in that stove.

Nevertheless, there I was on another particularly cold morning in my deer blind and the idea of having a warm fire burning was again, just too hard for me to resist. This time, however, I placed my rifle in a position where I could easily reach it and be ready if a buck showed up.

It didn't take me long before I had a pretty nice fire going in that wood stove. Only now, suddenly I realized that the smoke was not going up the rain gutter chimney. Instead, it was billowing out the door into the blind.

Evidently, over the previous winter, spring and summer, the spot where the rain gutter was connected to the small barrel stove had rusted out and the rain gutter had simply fallen into the barrel. It all happened so fast that I had to bail out of my deer blind.... In doing so, I made enough noise that would have scared away any deer that may have coming my way.

So there I was, again, sitting out in the cold waiting for the smoke to clear and wishing that I would have resisted the temptation to start a fire. Jesus was able to resist temptations in the wilderness because Jesus always considered the needs of others before his own needs.

As I reflect on my own experiences, I wonder, how often selfish actions leave us sitting out in the cold, waiting for the "smoke to clear?" The good news is that the smoke does clear. The wind of God's spirit, His love and His forgiveness clear the air for us in the same way that the wind on that cold winter day cleared the smoke out of my deer blind so that eventually I was able to get back to hunting.

I honestly don't remember if I saw any deer that day, or shot at anything. What I do remember is how warm the blind felt, even without a fire, after coming back in from sitting out in the cold. Even so, God calls us to return to him, over and over again. He waits patiently for us to empty ourselves of our own selfish and self-serving desires so that we can serve him by loving others.

But Jesus called them to him and said, "You know that the rulers of the Gentiles lord it over them, and their great ones are tyrants over them. ²⁶It will not be so among you; but whoever wishes to be great among you must be your servant, ²⁷and whoever wishes to be first among you must be your slave; ²⁸just as the Son of Man came not to be served but to serve, and to give his life a ransom for many." (Matthew 20:25-28)

PRAYER: Patient, loving and forgiving God, grant me the strength I need each day to overcome my own desires so that I might more effectively serve you by loving others. Clear away the smoke that is caused sin in my life and surround me with the warmth of your love. Amen.

BIG BUCK STORY – PART ONE

After hunting for enough years, I suspect that every hunter has at least one "Big Buck Story" to tell. I was fortunate enough to have my first "Big Buck Story" take place after only 8 years of hunting. The story begins as almost every hunting story begins with me sitting in my deer blind watching the power line opening for any sign of movement.

The power line opening faces to the south of my blind and occasionally I will turn to look behind me to the north and then slowly turn back to the south, checking out the tree line to the west, before continuing again mostly to pay attention to the power line to the south. This is the routine that I follow, hour after hour, day after day, when I am deer hunting.

Up to this point in my hunting experience, most of the deer that I have seen have come either from the south or the north and not so much from the east or the west. So, imagine my surprise on this day when, late in the afternoon, I saw some movement in the trees to the west as I was going through my routine of scanning those trees briefly before returning my attention the power line opening.

As I looked more closely at the movement, I could see it was a deer walking slowly through the trees. And then, I could see another deer, about 10 yards behind the first. I can remember how other hunters, when telling their "big buck stories," would say, "all I could see was antlers gleaming through the trees." And I would say, "Really?" Only now, here I am telling the same story….. All I could see were the antlers of this buck gleaming from the setting sun as it walked through the trees. I had no idea how big it was, but I knew it was a big buck.

My heart started pounding as I carefully shifted my rifle from the south window of my blind to the west window, trying not to make any noise. I located an opening in the trees behind the first deer and waited for the buck to walk into that opening. When it did, I put the cross hairs as best I could behind its front shoulder and squeezed the trigger.

When the gun went off, in a spit second, I saw the doe running in front of me to the south and I heard crashing in the trees to the west. And then, it was over. There was nothing but silence, except for the pounding of my heart.

They say that you are supposed to wait 10 minutes after shooting before leaving your blind to go look for your deer. I have to confess that I probably didn't wait that long. It was getting dark and I wanted to know if I hit the deer or not. So I marked the spot where I believed the buck was when I shot, and I went out to look for signs of blood.

I looked and looked and looked, but couldn't see any blood. Now it really was getting dark and so I started using my flashlight and kept looking until finally, I found a small spot of blood and a chunk of hair. "Ok," I thought to myself, "I hit it!" I marked that spot and decided to go back to the camp to get some help.

The guys at camp were more than willing to go with me back to that spot and begin looking for the buck. They brought lanterns and big flash lights to guide the way. Only, when we got there and I showed them the spot of blood and the tuft of hair, they said, "Is that it? Is that all you found?" Yep! They began looking and looking for quite a while and could find no more signs of blood.

Finally, they said, "It looks like you got 'buck fever' and jerked the rifle when you shot. You probably just grazed that buck in the brisket. He's long gone by now. Sorry…. Better luck next time."

With that we packed up our gear and all went back to the camp. I tried to shake it off, but I had a hard time not thinking about what had just happened. I went over it again and again in my mind and I couldn't convince myself that I had missed, that I had experienced what they call "buck fever."

There are many times in our lives when we have to face "reality" and accept things that we don't really want to accept. It is a bitter pill to swallow when life hands us failure and disappointment.

"Blessed are you," Jesus says, when you are hungry, meek, poor, and persecuted. Not because there is anything good about being hungry, meek, poor, or persecuted, but "Blessed are you," because even though the realities of life do not always give you what you want, God has promised to always give you what you need, namely, the assurance of His love, grace, mercy and forgiveness and the sure and certain hope that we have for eternal life.

As much as I hated to admit it, the experience of "almost getting" a big buck would need to be enough for me that day and I went to bed that night, thanking God for all of His greater blessings.

PRAYER: *Father in heaven, you know what we need more than we do. Give us each day those things as our daily bread even as you give us the patience and humility that we also need to accept the failures and disappointment that come our way. Amen*

BIG BUCK STORY – PART TWO

Learning how to accept disappointment and failure can be a daunting task and it usually doesn't happen overnight. It takes time to get over those painful feelings of what might have been but wasn't.

So it was on the morning after when I returned to my deer blind, all I could think about was what had happened the night before. There was no way that I was just going to sit there and try to keep hunting. I decided that as soon as it got light enough I was going to go and look for that "big buck."

I had to give it just one more try. I had no idea where to start since there was not blood trail or tracks to follow, so I decided to walk straight west until I reached a creek, that I knew ran through this property, "If I were a buck and I were wounded," I thought, "I would go and lay down next to the creek."

So that's what I did. And that's exactly where I found my "big buck", laying by the side of the creek! I can't begin to describe that experience. There he was, a ten point buck with thick antlers averaging 8 – 10 inches on each beam, with a 16 ½ inch spread on a perfectly symmetrical that had awesome looking brow tines. "Thank you very much!" That is the prayer I said in that moment. "Thank you God, very much!"

Of course, I know that God did not orchestrate the events of that day. God was with me, no doubt. Only, He was with me at first, helping me to try and deal with the disappointment and then, helping me to handle the success with humility.

I'm not so sure I did very well in either case. But, I also know that God is patient with me and loves me in spite of my own impatience and pride. And for that, I do say, "Thank you, God!"

"So if there is any encouragement in Christ, any comfort from love, any participation in the Spirit, any affection and sympathy, complete my joy by being of the same mind, having the same love, being in full accord and of one mind. Do nothing from selfish ambition or conceit, but in humility count others more significant than yourselves.

Let each of you look not only to his own interests, but also to the interests of others. Have this mind among yourselves which is yours in Christ Jesus, who though he was in the form of God, did not count equality with God a thing to be grasped, but emptied himself by taking the form of a servant, being born in the likeness of men. And being found in human form, he humbled himself by becoming obedient to the point of death, even death on a cross.

Therefore God has highly exalted him and bestowed on him the name that is above every name, so that at the name of Jesus every knee should bow in heaven and on earth and under the earth, and every tongue confess that Jesus Christ is Lord, to the glory of God the Father." (Philippians 2:1-11)

PRAYER: Great and loving God, continue to be patient with me as I seek to be a better person in all circumstances. Grow within me an ever greater awareness of what is most important in life, your love and the opportunities that you give for service in your kingdom. Amen.

BUCK SLAYER

Going to deer camp is an escape from reality that happens for me just one week out of every year. I enjoy the experience as it provides me with a greatly needed time for relaxation and re-creation so that I can return home ready to face the challenges of being a parish pastor.

I had returned from deer camp feeling pretty good about having bagged a "big buck." But, now that I was home, it didn't take very long for me to get back to the routine of work, planning meetings, writing sermons, preparing for bible studies etc.

I was home for lunch one day when there was a knock on the door. It was the mail man and he had a package in his hands. "I have a package for a Mr. Buck Slayer," he said. Well, I didn't know anyone named "Buck Slayer" and so I told him there was no one by that name living at this address. So, the mail man turned around and walked away, and I shut the door and went back to eating my lunch, thinking about what I had to next in order to get ready for a meeting a church that night.

Then, suddenly, it hit me, "buck slayer," that would be me! I went outside and literally chased down the mail man in his truck.

When I caught up with him I explained the confusion and told him that I had recently returned from deer camp and had, indeed, "slayed a big buck." He looked somewhat disinterested, but he gave me the package anyway.

When I got back home I opened the box to see that there were a pair of tennis shoes that I had left at camp and there was a note which read, "we thought you might need these before next year!"

Clearly my friends at deer camp were having some fun with me. And when it was all said and done I had to just sit down and laugh!

Sometimes we need some humor to break into our daily routines in order to remind us that God too has a sense of humor and He wants us to enjoy life as much as He wants us to live our lives by serving Him.

I am grateful for good friends and a good God who keeps me on my toes and who makes sure that I never take life's worries and problems too seriously.

"Rejoice in the Lord always; again I will say, rejoice. Let your reasonableness be known to everyone. The Lord is at hand; do not be anxious about anything, but in everything by prayer and supplication with thanksgiving let your requests be made know to God. And the peace of God, which surpasses all understanding, will guard your hearts and your minds in Christ Jesus." (Philippians 4:4-7)

PRAYER: Heavenly Father, give the ability to laugh enough each day so I might find, more than anything else, your peace in my heart and in my mind as I deal with the problems and worries of life. Amen.

BRINGING THE TROPHY HOME

The following year after I shot my 10 point buck, I accepted a call to pastor developer of a mission congregation in Alpine, CA, a suburb of San Diego. Before leaving deer camp that year I had also made arrangements to have my 10 point buck mounted by a taxidermist in the U.P.

Since I was now living in California, I told my friends in the U.P. that once the mount was completed they could just hang it at camp and I would come and visit it once a year.

To my surprise, later that summer, one of my hunting friends gave me a call and said that he was attending a seminar for work in San Diego and was hoping to spend a couple of days visiting with us there. I was delighted and happy to be able to be there to pick him up at the airport when he arrived.

As we stood by the luggage carrousel waiting for his luggage, a huge box came out on the moving carrousel and he said, "that's mine!" Sure enough, he had packed my Trophy Buck Mount in a box and had brought it with him to our home in California.

When we arrived at our home later that day, we hung the mount up over the fireplace in our living room before my wife came home from work. When she arrived and saw the 10 point buck hanging in our living room her first reaction was to say, "that's not staying there!"

My friend quickly told her that we had to bolt it to the wall (not true) and so it had to stay. She didn't like it, but accepted that explanation and my trophy buck hang in that spot for eight years until, having accepted another call to a church in Texas; we had to take it down. Now she was very surprised to see that it was just a single nail that held the mount to the wall.

Needless to say, when we arrived in Texas the trophy mount was delegated to be displayed in the garage. That's where it was for 10 years until I accepted another call to a congregation in Northern Wisconsin.

From the U.P. to California to Texas and now to Wisconsin, my trophy buck had made its rounds. But now that we were only an hour and a half away from deer camp I decided it was time to bring the trophy home.

Finally, 20 year later, I was able to bring the trophy with me to deer camp and hang it on a wall in the camp where it was shot! Being able to do that provided me with a certain feeling of peace. The traditions of deer camp and the respect that I have for the people that I hunt with, all contributed to that sense of peace.

"My peace I leave with you; my peace I give you," Jesus says, "not as the world gives do I give to you. Let not your hearts be troubled." (John 14:27)

There is no trophy that can replace the experience of being surrounded by the unconditional love of God, through the loving actions of faithful people. Seeing my trophy buck is now hanging at camp because that's where it belongs, in the same way that I also know "that's where I belong!"

PRAYER: Gracious God, I thank you for the gift of faithful people throughout my life who have accepted me for who I am and who have offered their love to me without reservation. Allow your love to flow through me in such a way that others might feel your peace, also in my presence. Amen.

A STICKY SITUATION

Normally, when I am deer hunting, I am sitting in a deer blind that sits on the ground. But occasionally, I take advantage of the opportunity to sit in a tree stand, when one of the other hunters offers the invitation.

On this particular occasion, one of the other hunters had to back home a little earlier than usual and he had been seeing deer just about every day from his tree stand. I, on the other hand, had not seen any deer at all to that point in the season, so I was more than willing to accept his invitation to sit in his tree stand on the morning when he would be gone.

It just so happened, that it was very cold and windy on that morning when I climbed into the tree stand just before sunrise. I sat there for two hours, freezing and wondering why and the world I wasn't sitting in my cozy, warm deer stand on the ground.

And then, I noticed some movement in the marsh grass to my left. When I looked I could see a deer running through the marsh and behind it was a buck. I had no idea how big of a buck; I could only see that its antlers were outside of its ears as his head bounded up and down through the tall marsh grass.

I readied my rifle and went to turn left so that I could assume a shooting position when, all of a sudden, I realized that I couldn't move. My rear end was stuck to the seat. Evidently pitch from the pine tree had been dripping on the seat and the heat from my rear end and warmed it up enough so that it became like glue, holding me tight to the chair.

"You've got to be kidding me," I thought to myself as I watched that buck run through the marsh grass, but could get myself in a position to shoot.

I have been stuck before, but never like that. I have been stuck in the mud, stuck in the snow, and even "stuck in a rut," metaphorically speaking. Usually, "being stuck" is not the problem, it's "getting unstuck" that is the problem.

It takes effort and energy to get unstuck from most situations and sometimes we just don't have the will power even try. Instead we may just sit back and feel sorry for ourselves and say, "oh well, I'm stuck, not much I can do about it."

The truth is this is how it can be in our relationship with God. We get stuck in a routine of going to church, saying our prayers, maybe reading our bible once in a while or attending a bible study, but beyond that, there's not much movement. We feel like our faith journey isn't really going anywhere because we don't make the effort to get "unstuck!"

When Jesus left his disciples, he told them, "Go and make disciples of all nations!" And what did they do. They went right back to fishing. They were stuck. But Jesus did not give up on them. He appeared to them again, on the sea shore and reminded them what it was they were called to do as people of faith:

"When they had finished breakfast, Jesus said to Simon Peter, "Simon son of John, do you love me more than these?" He said to him, "Yes, Lord; you know that I love you." Jesus said to him, "Feed my lambs." 16A second time he said to him, "Simon son of John, do you love me?" He said to him, "Yes, Lord; you know that I love you." Jesus said to him, "Tend my sheep." 17He said to him the third time, "Simon son of John, do you love me?" Peter felt hurt because he said to him the third time, "Do you love me?" And he said to him, "Lord, you know everything; you know that I love you." Jesus said to him, "Feed my sheep." (John 21:15-17)

In other words, get off your duff and make a difference by sharing the bread of life with others! Jesus did not give up on his disciples and He does not give up on us either. God is patient, but God is also persistent!

That morning in the tree blind, stuck to my seat, I was frustrated for a moment, but the sight of that buck running through the marsh grass compelled me to do something. I set my rifle on my lap and I literally peeled my rear end off of the seat so that I could move. I then re-located where the buck was and just before it reached the trees on the other side of the Marsh, I took a shot. I ended up getting a nice 5 point buck, because I didn't give up.

PRAYER: *Thank you God for being so patient and so persistent with me. Open my ears so that can hear your voice calling me to feed your sheep. Open my eyes so that I can see the mission that you have given me to do each day and Open my heart so that I will not give up, but will instead be compelled to serve you by loving others. Amen.*

THE BUCK ALARM

Usually, when it's deer season, I don't need a "wake-up call." The excitement and anticipation that precedes the beginning of hunting season is enough to wake me up every morning at 5 am. This is true for at least the first three days of hunting season.

As the season goes on however, it can get harder and harder to get out of bed that early. This is particularly true when you have already been successful. If you have a buck, hanging on the buck pole, the motivation for getting up early starts to fade pretty fast. And even if you are not successful, especially if you have not even seen any signs of deer moving, day after day after day, it can become so frustrating that you lose your mental commitment to even want to get up and sit out in the cold.

It happened to be that kind of year for me when after the third day of deer hunting I announced that I would not be getting up the next morning. "I'm taking the morning off tomorrow," I said, "I need a morning to just sleep in!" I heard the other hunters get up in the morning, but I just turned around in my bunk and went back to sleep.

It was around 8:00 in the morning when I heard someone, the wife of the owner of the camp, yell out, "Does anyone want to shoot a buck this morning?" I remember myself thinking at that moment, "No, I already told everybody I'm not getting up." But then the she said again, "Does anyone want to shoot a buck this morning, because there's one standing here right behind the camp!" Suddenly, she had my attention.

I got up and went to look out the back window of the camp, still wearing only my long underwear, and sure enough there was a six point buck just standing there about 50 yards behind the camp. "Get your rifle," she said, "you can shoot out of our bedroom window."

I was just a little dazed and confused but I obediently went into the bunk room and took my rifle out of its case. I then had to find my hunting jacket in order to get some shells from its pocket. "Hurry up;" she said again, "it's not going to stand there all day!"

Eventually, I made my way to their bedroom window and opened it up enough so that I could point my rifle barrel out, I located the buck, who by this time had begun to walk away from camp towards the woods, and I took a shot. "Did you get it?" She asked, and I responded, "I don't know, I think so."

I then got dressed and together we went to look for the buck and we found it laying pretty much right where it was when I shot.

Who would have thought that I would ever shoot a buck before getting dressed in the morning? I thanked her for being my "Buck Alarm" that morning and I still marvel at how the most unbelievable things happen at deer camp.

Since then, I have also had opportunities to marvel at some of the most unbelievable things happen in God's Kingdom when we allow ourselves to listen to God's voice calling us to "get up and get going!" Jesus said to His disciples, "The harvest is plentiful but the laborers are few." And now I remember a popular hymn that was based on Jesus' words:

Hark! the voice of Jesus crying,
"Who will go and work today?
Fields are white and harvests waiting;
Who will bear the sheave away?"
Loud and long the Master calleth;
Rich reward He offers free;
Who will answer, gladly saying,
"Here am I; send me, send me"?

PRAYER: Heavenly Father, rouse me from the slumber of complacency and frustration and waken me to the voice of your call. Never let me oversleep or overlook an opportunity to proclaim the power of your love for all people. Give me courage to faith to respond always, "Here am I, send me!" AMEN.

LIGHTING ANOTHER FIRE!

When I go to the U.P. for deer hunting I hunt at two different deer camps. For the first half of the week, I hunt with one group at their camp and then for the second half of the week I hunt with another group at their camp. They are all great friends and I have been keeping this schedule for over 30 years.

On one of those days when I make the transition from one camp to another, I arrived at the second camp only to discover that the owner of the camp and my good friend had to leave earlier that day for a meeting in Minnesota, but that he would be back before I left. His brother was there to greet me and told me that before my good friend had left, he wanted him to tell me that I was welcome to go ahead and hunt in his blind.

Now that is quite a privilege, to be invited to hunt in the blind of the owner of the camp. As you might expect, his blind was located in one of the prime locations for seeing bucks.

Naturally, I was grateful for the opportunity. The next morning I rode out with another hunter who dropped me off by a logging road that I would walk on in order to get to my friends blind. Because it was very cold that morning, the other hunter told me before dropping me off that he was only going to sit until 8 am and then he was going back to camp. I agreed on the plan and told him to go ahead and drive in to pick me up at 8 am.

I'll have to admit that I was somewhat skeptical that my invitation to sit in this blind was legitimate. So I thought, at least, I would just sit there for a little bit and then leave. These were the days when blinds were not insulated and there were no "Mr. Buddy" propane heaters. However, when I got there, I noticed that there was a "Coleman" oil heater sitting in the corner of this blind.

It was cold and the wind was blowing and once again, it didn't take me long to decide to try and get this heater going. My heart wasn't exactly into actually hunting that morning anyway because of my doubts about my friend actually wanting that to happen.

So, I turned on my flash light to read the directions. They said that I should turn the heater upside down for 5 seconds and then set it up right again and that I should see a spot of oil on the burning surface "about the size of a quarter."

I turned the heater upside down and counted out 5 seconds and then I looked for the spot of oil, but there wasn't one. I didn't see anything. So….. I turned it upside down again and counted another 5 seconds before turning it upright and looking again. Now there was a spot of oil, only it wasn't the size of a quarter, it was the size of a pancake!

Never having used one of these heaters before, I decided to go ahead and light the match. When I touched the match to the oil spot I had a big surprise. A flame shot up about four feet high, almost touching the roof of the blind. I had to jump out of this small blind to avoid catching on fire myself.

There I was, once again, out in the cold, only this time I wasn't waiting for smoke to clear, I was waiting for flames to subside! Now here's the best part. I had made so much noise, lighting that fire, jumping out of the blind and then getting back into the blind that by the time I did get back in the blind and had the heater situation under control I pretty much had given up on any idea of actually hunting that morning.

Instead, I took off my boots and warmed my feet by the heater, waiting for 8 am to come so that I could go back to camp.

It was about 7:45 am when I started putting my boots back on and I noticed some movement in front of me, a deer running through the hard woods. And then, sure enough there was another deer running behind it, a buck. I could see that it had a rack. Not a big rack, but a definite rack.

Instinctively, I reached for my rifle, put it out the window and picked an opening in the trees where the buck was heading. When I saw brown in my scope, I pulled the trigger.

The next thing I knew was that there were no more deer anywhere in front of me. Since there was a lot of snow on the ground that year, I went out to check for any signs of blood and found nothing.

About that time, my other friend from camp pulled up with his truck to pick me up. "I heard you shoot," he said, "did you get it?" I said, "I don't think so, it was a buck, but I couldn't see any blood and there are tons of deer tracks in the snow. "Let's go back to camp and get "Sonny," if you hit that buck, he'll be the one to track it." "Sonny" was, in fact, the brother of my friend who had told me I had his permission to hunt in his blind.

When he heard that I had shot at a buck. He was excited. He thought it would be great fun to tell his brother that the "preacher" had shot a buck while sitting in his blind.

Sure enough, when we got back to the area where I had shot, Jr. began tracking. I was skeptical, but it wasn't long before I heard him yell, "here it is!" Believe it or not, there was an eight point buck lying on the ground, shot through the heart! "Nice shot preacher," he said. He was so happy that he even field dressed the deer for me and led the celebration when we got back to camp.

This story has been told and retold by my friend whose blind it was where I shot this buck. He had never given anyone permission for anyone, including me, to hunt off of his blind that day. "I can't believe that you would believe Jr". he would say. "And then to top it off you almost burned my blind to the ground!" This is what makes deer camp so enjoyable. The good humor, the amazing stories and the many, many times that you get to tell them.

If only we were so excited about telling the story of God's Love. If only we were so "on fire" for those opportunities that we have to witness to the grace, love and mercy of God.

"When he (Jesus) was at the table with them, he took bread, blessed and broke it, and gave it to them. [31]Then their eyes were opened, and they recognized him; and he vanished from their sight. [32]They said to each other, "Were not our hearts burning within us while he was talking to us on the road, while he was opening the scriptures to us?" (Luke 24:30-32)

PRAYER: Great and loving God. I thank you for the friendships and comradery of deer camp. I thank you for great stories and opportunities to tell them. Most of all I thank you for the greatest story of all, the story of your love. Set my heart on fire to tell that story over and over again so that others too might celebrate the gift of eternal joy. AMEN.

THE BUCK THAT GOT AWAY

Every deer hunter has stories to tell. Some of the stories are stories of celebration that recount the events of a successful hunt. Some of the stories are humorous anecdotes that recount the crazy and unpredictable events that take place at deer camp. Some of the stories are stories that are only told at deer camp and nowhere else.

And then there are those stories that nobody actually wants to tell, stories of failure.

It has been my usual custom to stop off at a rifle range sometime before the deer season starts in order to sight in my rifle. Typically, my rifle is always sighted in with only minor adjustments needed from year to year. In this particular year, for whatever reason, I chose not to stop and sight my rifle in.

So it was, on the first day of season, I was sitting in my deer blind as usual, looking down the power line to the south of my blind. It was about three o'clock in the afternoon and the sun was shining bright. I had my ear plugs in, listening to a local radio station and I was smoking a cigar with my rifle at hand, leaning up against a corner of the blind.

For a brief moment I was looking toward the west to see if there was any movement there and then I turned back to the south and there he was, the biggest buck I have ever seen outside of a magazine. He was just standing there about 50 yards to the south of my blind and he wasn't even looking in my direction. He was looking to the west.

I couldn't believe what I was seeing. I took my ear plugs out, put down my cigar and lifted my rifle to a position through the blind window to take aim.

As I tried to focus my scope on the buck, I realized that because the sun was shining so bright, I could not see the cross hairs in the scope. I could see the buck, still standing there, but I couldn't bring the cross hairs into focus.

For a moment, I was confused and tried my best to adjust the position of the scope against my eye, but nothing seemed to work. And then, the buck moved.

It didn't run. It didn't jump. It didn't make any sudden movement. It just took one step forward and I panicked. I took a shot. In an instant that buck was now bounding to the south away from me. I can still picture his majestic rack bouncing up and down as he disappeared from my sight. He was gone!

What made matters even worse was the fact that when I went to look to see if there were any signs of blood, instead of finding blood I found hair, lots and lots of hair. Clearly I had hit that buck, but as it was running it didn't look like it had been hit.

My first thought was that I had "gut shot" him. Which is not good, but at least there would be a chance they I could still find him. A deer that has been gut shot can run for a long ways, so I decided not to go looking for him right away. My hope was that he would go into the marsh and find someplace to lie down and that I would find him there after he had died.

So I waited, going over the place where I found hair with a "fine tooth comb" looking for any signs of blood. Finally, after I could wait no longer, (probably about ½ hour) I started walking into the marsh hoping to find a blood trail there. It was getting dark and I didn't have very long to look. I found nothing. I went back to camp and told this sad story to the other hunters.

We'll go looking tomorrow morning they said. And so we did. Because of my previous experience with finding the Big Buck that I had shot on the following morning, I still had high hopes that I would find this buck too. However, that didn't happen. I looked high and low, up and down all over that marsh for the next two days until I was convinced that I hadn't "gut shot" the buck but I must have grazed on its underbelly.

I took my rifle out and set up a target to make sure it was sighted in and, sure enough, it wasn't. It was shooting about 8 inches low.

So there it is. That's my story and to be honest with you, just writing it out still feels kind of painful. I was so disappointed in myself. To be even more honest, I have to tell you that this is not the first time I've been disappointed in myself. There have been other times, having nothing to do with deer hunting, when my actions, in retrospect have been disappointing.

The amazing thing about deer camp is that, although the other hunters may give you hard time about little things, like smoking yourself out of a blind or shooting a buck with a coffee thermos cover on its hoof, when it comes to those moments when your spirit is being crushed, somehow they know that what is needed is not humor, but comfort and encouragement.

"Come to me," Jesus says, *"all you who are weak and heavily burdened, and I will give you rest…… for my yoke is easy and my burden is light!" (Matthew 11:28)*

At the end of the day, we can take all of our heavy burdens and lay them at the feet of Jesus, who understands our pain, and who offers his comfort and encouragement.

PRAYER: Understanding and merciful God, thank you for your constant love and endless compassion. Lift my spirit when it is down with the assurance of your presence and the certainty of your promise that in all things you are with me. AMEN.

A NICE BUCK FOR A GOOD FRIEND

Although I have lived in many different states, including Nebraska, Indiana, Missouri, Minnesota, Michigan, Wisconsin, California and Texas, I have hunted pretty much exclusively in the U.P. of Michigan.

There were, however, a couple of occasions when I had the opportunity to go deer hunting outside of the U.P. The most notable of those occasions, took place in Texas. Winston was an older member of our congregation who used to stop by the church office every Monday morning because his wife, Betty, was one of the volunteers who came in on Mondays to count the previous Sunday's offerings.

While Betty was in the church library with a few other ladies, counting the offerings, Winston would come to my office and we would talk about deer hunting. He knew that I went to the U.P. of Michigan every November and he was interested in hearing from me what deer hunting was like "up there!" Winston also was a deer hunter. He and another member of our congregation had been hunting together for many years. Naturally, I got to hear his stories also, about deer hunting in Texas.

The day came, however, when Winston's deer hunting partner passed away. It wasn't long after I had conducted the funeral service for his friend that Winston was sitting in my office on a Monday morning lamenting the fact that he "probably wouldn't be going deer hunting anymore." "I have no one to go hunting with," he said.

Since I knew that the dates for deer hunting in Texas were different than the dates in Michigan, I said, "How about if I went hunting with you." "Really," he replied, "you'd be willing to do that?" "Sure," I said, "why not, I think it would fun to try hunting in Texas." "Well, ok," he said, "I'll put in an application for us for the first available week." And so he did.

The time came for Winston and I to go deer hunting together. The place where we would be hunting was actually a state wildlife preserve where you applied for a hunting site and were assigned a specific area within the reserve where you could hunt. We drove down to the state park and got ourselves a motel for the night and then we went out to the reserve and signed ourselves in, obtaining a map of the area where we would be hunting the next morning.

Early that next morning, we made our way out to the area. Winston parked his truck at a designated parking area nearby and we agreed on the spots where we would each be hunting. Winston would be about 100 yards away from where I would be hunting on the other side of a ridge.

I settled into a make shift blind, flanked by three trees and sitting on a rock. I sat there for maybe an hour or so, when suddenly I heard a car horn beeping. It sounded like it was coming from Winston's truck, so I went to see what was going on.

Sure enough, there was Winston standing outside of his truck with his hand inside the window beeping the horn. When he saw me coming towards the truck he said, "Oh, there you are. I thought maybe you got lost." That was Winston.

What he enjoyed about deer hunting most of all, was talking, not hunting. So we talked about where we were, and what we hadn't seen, and what we would do next. That's the way those three days of hunting in Texas were like. No deer, but good conversations.

It was a couple of years later that Winston died. After the funeral service, I had a chance to talk to his son, who had a PhD. In Nuclear Science and was a professor at a college. His son thanked me for being a good friend to his dad. He said, "I heard you even went hunting with him." "Yes, I did," I replied, "and I had a great time. I will miss your dad."

Now the day came when I had accepted a call to a different congregation and we were moving back to Wisconsin. The moving truck was parked outside of our home in Texas and it was being loaded up. We would be driving out of time later that afternoon, leaving Texas behind.

A car pulled up and parked behind the moving truck. I didn't recognize the car until I saw that it was Winston's son, getting out of the car with a rifle case in his hands. "Pastor," he said, "I'm glad I caught you before you left town. This is my dad's hunting rifle and I want you to have it."

"Oh wow," I said, "Thank you, but I really can't accept a gift like that you should keep it yourself." "No," he replied, "I know how much my dad enjoyed going hunting with you and I don't hunt. I think my dad would be happy knowing that you are still hunting with his rifle. Please accept this gift!"
How could I refuse? So I gratefully accepted the gift and took Winston's rifle, a Winchester, Model 70, 270, with me to Wisconsin.

That November, when I made my way to the U.P. for deer hunting, I decided that I would hunt with Winston's rifle. I couldn't help but think of my friend Winston as I sat in my Michigan deer blind holding his rifle. The third day of the season, early in the morning, I saw some movement in the power line to my south. I kept looking and saw a buck, lift its head sot that I could see it had a nice rack, but all I could see was its head and its neck.

I waited for a few minutes to see if it would move out in the clear, but it didn't. I finally decided that if I wanted to shoot that buck, I would have to take a neck shot. So the next time it lifted its head, I placed the cross hairs of that Winchester 70, 270 on its neck and pulled the trigger. Down it went.

When I walked over to where the deer was laying I could see that it was a very nice 8 point buck! "Thank you Winston," I said. Later I had a picture taken with me holding Winston's rifle and standing over that 8 point buck. I sent the picture to Winston's son thanking him again for the gift of his dad's rifle.

There is more to life than just deer hunting, but there is also more to deer hunting than just deer hunting.

[7]So again Jesus said to them, "Very truly, I tell you, I am the gate for the sheep. [8]All who came before me are thieves and bandits; but the sheep did not listen to them. [9]I am the gate. Whoever enters by me will be saved, and will come in and go out and find pasture. [10]The thief comes only to steal and kill and destroy. I came that they may have life, and have it abundantly. (John 10:7-10)

An abundant life, is a life filled with the joy of good friends and with whom you can share meaningful conversation of faith and experience together the unconditional love of God…..even while deer hunting!

PRAYER: Eternal God, thank you for the gift of good friends and for the opportunities that we have to encourage and support one another. Thank you also for the sure and certain hope that we have for eternal life even as we celebrate the abundance of the life we share together now. Amen.

THE BUCK THAT WASN'T A BUCK

There was a time when the rule at deer camp was, "if it's brown, it's down!" Those days have long since gone. The rule at deer camp these days is defined by "Quality Deer Management" or in other words, "Let it go and let it grow!"

At the deer camps where I hunt Quality Deer Management, or as we call it, QDM, simply means that unless the buck has at least 3 points on one beam, then you should let it go.

I'll have to admit that it has taken me a while to get used to this method of hunting. When I see a buck, my instinct is to see if I can get a shot at it. However, over time, I have become more and more conscience of QDM and have, in fact, let a number of bucks go by, because they did not meet the QDM standards.

So it was on one day at deer camp, I was sitting on a blind in the hard woods behind the camp at the second deer camp where I hunt. I hadn't seen any deer and it was getting dark.

When you sitting in the woods, and it starts to get dark, it doesn't usually take very long before it is dark. I was just about to call it a day when I saw something move in the trees about 50 yards to the west of where I was sitting. I looked through the scope and saw a deer standing behind a tree. I could see its body, but I couldn't see its head because it was grazing on something on the ground.

I waited for it to lift its head. Finally, it lifted its head and I could see that there was a rack. But then, it quickly put its head back down. I thought to myself, "that deer is a buck….. I'm pretty sure." But I didn't get a close enough look to see if it met QDM standards.

So, I waited again for it to lift its head. As I am waiting, of course, it is getting darker and darker. Finally it lifted its head again, and I was certain this time that this buck had a rack and that it had at least 3 points on one side.

As it put its head back down, I carefully aimed to take a shot at its neck which was the only part of this deer that I could still see. I pulled the trigger and when the shot went off, I immediately saw 3 white tails running away from that spot!

I was surprised, to say the least. I thought there was only one deer out there. Now it really was dark and since I was in the woods in a place where I wasn't all that familiar with the terrain, I decided to go back to camp and get some help before looking for the deer I had shot.

I explained what happened at camp and a group of the other hunters went with me to see what we could find. It wasn't long before one of the group shouted out, "I've got blood!" He then, followed that trail of blood for a short distance before saying, "Here it is!" I was excited.

I couldn't wait to see how big this buck really was. And then, when I got to the spot where the deer was laying, I couldn't believe what I saw. It wasn't a buck at all, it was a doe! "That's not the deer I shot," I said.

"Really," the hunter who had found the deer replied, "well, this is the deer that ran bleeding from the spot where you just told us you were aiming!" I didn't know what to say. "Do you think," I continued, "that this deer was standing in front of the buck that I saw, and when I shot at the buck, I hit this doe instead?"

"Well, I suppose that could have happened," he replied, "highly unlikely....but possible." We continued to look for any other signs of blood that might indicate that I shot through this doe and still may have hit the buck.

In the end, the only deer we found was that doe. Fortunately, I did have a doe tag and I field dressed the doe while the other hunters held their lights and made subtle comments about my ability to tell the difference between a buck and a doe.

There were a lot of lessons to be learned again from this experience. The most important of them for me was this: When it's too dark to know for sure, don't shoot!"

"Jesus said to them, "The light is with you for a little longer. Walk while you have the light, so that the darkness may not overtake you. If you walk in the darkness, you do not know where you are going. ³⁶While you have the light, believe in the light, so that you may become children of light." (John 12:35, 36)

PRAYER: God of light and love, thank you for sending your Son, Jesus to be the light of the world, to show me the way of grace, love, mercy and compassion. Draw me each day ever into His light and give me patience, strength and courage to resist the darkness of the world that all too quickly falls upon me. AMEN

BUILDING A NEW BLIND

For over twenty-five years, I had been privileged to sit in a blind that was built especially for me by the patriarch of the family who owns the camp. Elmer was a small man with a huge heart and a great love for God. He didn't believe in wasting, time, materiel or money on things that weren't necessary, but he did believe in being generous when it came to the relationships that he shared with both people and with God.

I am grateful for Elmer, for the friendship that we shared and for the blind that he built for me.

Eventually, however, I came to the conclusion that the time had come for me to build a new blind. Although Elmer's blind had served me well for many years, it was now weathered and worn. Not to mention the fact that it was very small, making it difficult to move around inside of it without making noise.

I mentioned, one day, to the owner of the camp that I was thinking about building a new blind. He said, "I was wondering how long you were going to keep on sitting in that little blind that dad built." He went on to say that whenever I wanted to start building a new blind, he would help.

So we decided that that next summer, in advance of the deer season, I would come up to camp for a few days and we would build a new blind. So it was, I showed up at camp in August and began the project.

Elmer's son, the owner of the camp, told me that I should go with one of the other hunters, who was also at camp at that time and who was willing to help, so that we could load up some lumber that he had standing in the woods.

We ended up coming back with a load of lumber and quickly began putting together my plan for a new blind. We built the blind at camp deciding that when it was completed we would just pick it up with a front end loader on a tractor and carry it to the spot where I hunt where we would just set it in the place that I wanted it to be.

The blind ended up being five feet square and about six feet tall. It has windows on each side that open and close, an actual door that opens and shuts and a roof that is covered with a rubber mat so that it won't leak. It is insulated with 1" Styrofoam and has a carpeted floor. It also has a built in shelf for my rifle.

Once it was in place, I added a propane fueled heater that has electronic ignition and an upholstered chair that swivels. I then completed the project by painting the outside of blind in a camouflage pattern so that it blends easily into the background of the woods. "Now that's a blind," I thought, as I stood back and admired the completed project. I have been hunting in this new blind now for two years and have been successful each year.

The first year, I shot a nice eight point buck! Did the new blind contribute to this success? The answer is, probably not. The old blind was always a pretty successful blind. Building a new blind for me is more a celebration of the relationships that have been built at deer camp over the years. It is comfortable, warm and strong, in the same way that the relationships I share with the members of deer camp are also. As time goes by, things change.

Hopefully those changes are mostly positive. Being generous, genuine and gracious are the qualities needed for building comfortable, warm and strong relationships both with other people and even with God.

"Do not let your hearts be troubled. Believe in God, believe also in me. ²In my Father's house there are many dwelling places. If it were not so, would I have told you that I go to prepare a place for you? ³And if I go and prepare a place for you, I will come again and will take you to myself, so that where I am, there you may be also." (John 14:1-3)

The good news is that God has already provided all of these building materials for us by sending His Son, Jesus Christ to show us who he really is, a God of love, to pour out his love for us on the cross, and to give us the gift of eternal life.

PRAYER: Loving, generous and gracious God, thank you for providing everything needed for building relationships with others even as you have built the most important relationship of all with me through your Son, Jesus Christ. Help me each day to use the gifts of your love in such a way so that I too might be genuine, generous and gracious with others. Amen.

MR. "SPIKEY"

Although my son, Tony, when he was only 8 year old, was able to participate in the shooting of my very first deer, he never did have an opportunity to go deer hunting himself until 29 years later when he was 37 years old. It wasn't because Tony didn't want to go deer hunting it was a combination of life circumstances and geography that made it difficult to actually do so.

Finally, when the day came that he told me he was ready to go deer hunting with me, I was excited about the idea of spending some father-son time with Tony at deer camp! That first year at camp Tony fit right in with the rest of the crew and we all had a great time. Tony helped another hunter track a buck and drag it out of the swamp and he sat for hours in a deer blind himself, waiting for this own opportunity to come, which, unfortunately did not happen that year.

Still, Tony was enthused and anxious to come back and try again the next year. When next year came around, the owner of the camp reminded Tony, "if you're shooting your first buck any legal buck will do, but after that it has to meet QDM standards. (3pts. Or better on one side)

After a couple of days of hunting, my friend, the owner of the camp, and I decided that we would go and post on some property that was a little further away from came than normal for our evening post. I sat on one edge of the property and he sat on the other edge. We kept in communication through text messages on our cell phones.

We were far enough away from the camp; however, that if Tony shot from where he was sitting we would not be able to hear that shot. So, I was wondering, and hoping that Tony might shoot something that night. As it got dark, and my friend and I were heading in from our blinds, I received a text message from my son, it read: "I just shot a buck!" I was excited.

I showed the text message to my friend, and he said, "Good for Tony, way to go!" I quickly texted Tony back saying, "Congratulations! How big?" He responded. "I shot a buck."

"Ok," I thought, "No problem!" We made it back to camp and waited for Tony to show up with his buck. He was being assisted in the field dressing process by two of my friend's sons. It ended up being quite a while before they finally showed up at camp.

There was a big smile on Tony's face, a big cigar in his mouth, and the smallest buck I have ever seen in my life, laying in the back of a pick-up truck. One of the other hunters from our group went over to take a look and said, "He shot 'Mr. Spikey!"

It seems that this little buck had been making the rounds that season and this particular hunter had nick named him "Mr. Spikey." It was an appropriate nick name because this buck only had one horn, barely 4 inches high.

Nevertheless, Tony was thrilled to tell his story. "It was getting dark," he said, "and I saw something moving into the opening, when I held up my rifle, all I could see was horns!" "You mean horn," one of the other hunters interjected, and we all laughed!

"I saw that it was a buck," Tony continued, "and I decided to shoot it." "When I pulled the trigger, BAM!, down it went!"

"Congratulations!" My friend shouted out, "It's time to celebrate Tony's first buck!" And so we did. And it was a great night of celebration for all of us.

"With what can we compare the kingdom of God, or what parable will we use for it? ³¹It is like a mustard seed, which, when sown upon the ground, is the smallest of all the seeds on earth; ³²yet when it is sown it grows up and becomes the greatest of all shrubs, and puts forth large branches, so that the birds of the air can make nests in its shade." (Mark 4:30-32)

The size of a buck, or a size of the bank account, or the size of any "thing" that we might aspire to obtain in life, never ends up being nearly as important as the size of one's heart and the genuine love and compassion that is shared between friends.

So Jesus also reminds us that the "least" will become great and the "last" will become first in His Kingdom.

PRAYER: Loving God, Help me always to keep my mind set on what is "great" in this world, but rather on the greatness of you love for me and for all people. Increase my own capacity for loving others, even as you fill me each day with the fullness and joy of your kingdom! Amen.

SWITCHING AMMUNITION

From past experience, I have learned how important it is to sight your rifle in every year. The year that my son, Tony, was going to join me at deer camp I needed to sight in two rifles, one for me, my Winchester 70/270, and one for Tony, my Remington Game Master 30-06.

I stopped at the rifle range on my way to camp and proceeded to sight in the Winchester 270 first. After three or four shots I was confident that it was sighted in. So then, I took out the Remington 30-06. I fired three rounds at a target 100 yards away.

When I turned to ask the range attendant what my grouping looked like, he said, "you didn't even hit the paper." "What?" I couldn't believe what he was telling me. "Try a target at 50 yards," he said. So I did. Still, none of my shots hit the paper even at 50 yards.

"Something must be really wrong," I said. The range attendant came out and checked my scope to see if it was loose, but no, it was fine. "What kind of ammunition are you using," he asked. And then, it hit me. I had switched rifles, but I hadn't switched ammunition.

I was firing 270 shells out of a 30-06 barrel! No wonder I couldn't hit anything. The 270 bullets were just tumbling out of the barrel of the rifle out of control.

Once I took out my box of 30-06 shells and put them in the Remington 30-06, not only did I hit the paper, I was "dead on," no adjustments needed to be made. Here is an important lesson I learned on that day. Rifles are built to fire ammunition that was specifically designed for them.

When God created us, He created us in a certain way, to be and act in certain ways in relationship with Him and in relationship with each other. The problem is, because of sin, we end up very often tumbling through life out of control. Instead of being generous, loving and forgiving, we are too often selfish, fearful and resentful. It is worth noting that the Greek word for "sin" can actually be literally translated "to miss the target!"

It is as if we have loaded the wrong kind of ammunition in our rifle. Certainly that's not the way God intended it to be.

"So God created humankind in his image, in the image of God he created them; male and female he created them." (Genesis 1:27)

God created us to be like Him. And then, God sent Jesus to come into the world in order to set things right, to switch what was wrong with what is right, to put "His right Spirit within us," so that we will never run out again.

PRAYER: Creator God, I thank you for the goodness of your creation and even more so, for the generosity of your love that has overcome the power of sin within us. Keep me ever mindful of who I am, a child of God, created in your own image, and give me the strength of your Spirit so that I all that I do, I might stay on target. Amen.

LOCKED IN THE BLIND

It was one of those years when I was seeing absolutely nothing from my blind. I had sat for three days without seeing so much as a single deer. As I wondered out loud, "whether it made any sense for me to go sit in that blind for a fourth day," one of the other hunters told me that he had to go home that night and would not be back for the morning hunt. "If you want to sit in my blind, you're welcome to do so," he said. "Really," I replied, "if you don't mind, I think that is what I would like to do."

That next morning I made my way to his blind. It was a nice blind. In fact, when I eventually built my new blind, I modeled it after this blind. The only difference being, this blind was built 25 feet in the air. It was nestled like a tree house between several large trees on the edge of a marsh. I climbed the ladder to get into the blind, I turned the block of wood that was holding the door shut from the outside, I opened the door, went into the blind, shut the door and made myself at home.

It was a beautiful day, there was snow on the ground, the sun was shining and there was no wind. I kept the windows open, sat back in his swivel chair and enjoyed the view.

After about an hour of watching the sun rise and checking out the different scenery, I saw a deer running from behind where I was sitting out into the marsh in front of me. I readied my rifle, hoping a buck would be chasing that deer.

Sure enough, here came a buck, chasing that doe. I took aim and fired and down he went. Because he was now lying in the tall marsh grass, I couldn't actually see him on the ground. I kept my rifle aimed on the spot in case he might jump up. But no, he was down.

After about 15 minutes of watching and waiting, I finally relaxed and put my rifle down. I wasn't sure how big he was but I knew he met DQM standards so I lit up a cigar to celebrate and gathered my things together to go and look at my buck.

When I went to open the door of the blind, however, it wouldn't open. The wood block that I had turned to open the door when I entered the blind had fallen shut again and I was now locked in the blind!

I tried everything I could. I shook the door, I leaned out of the windows as far as I could, but there was nothing that I could do to move that block of wood. I even thought about kicking the door open, but since it was not "my blind" I decided that was not a good idea.

Instead, I finally decided that the only way out was to use my cell phone in order to call for help. If you call your friends in deer camp to tell them that you've locked yourself in a deer blind, you should expect a certain amount of good natured ridicule to be thrown in your direction. I knew that, and so I also prepared myself for whatever might follow.

I spoke to the wife of the owner of the camp. I told her that I had good news and I had bad news. "The good news," I said, is that I shot a buck. "Congratulations," she replied, "what's the bad news?" "The bad news," I replied, "is that I have somehow locked myself in this blind and I can't get out. I need someone to come and let me out."

"You did what," she exclaimed. And then she started laughing. "Don't worry help is on the way." Before long I heard the sound of four-wheelers in the distance. Here came a parade of people on four wheelers all wanting to see this ridiculous situation that I had gotten myself into.

After laughing at me for a few minutes, one of my friends finally crawled up and unlocked the door so that I could exit the blind. "Now let's go see that buck you shot," he said. I took them to the place that I had marked where the buck had fallen and there was a nice 7 point buck. "I'll take that," I said and before you knew it the laughter had turned into celebration.

"For everything there is a season, and a time for every matter under heaven: [2]a time to be born, and a time to die; a time to plant, and a time to pluck up what is planted; [3]a time to kill, and a time to heal; a time to break down, and a time to build up;[4]a time to weep, and a time to laugh; a time to mourn, and a time to dance;" (Ecclesiastes 3:1-4)

PRAYER: God of joy and celebration, thank you for giving me the ability to laugh at myself and to acknowledge that there are times in life when it is important to do so. Thank you for the willingness of friends who are there to help when help is needed. Continue to shape me in such a way so that at all times and in all circumstances I might be, more than anything else, grateful for you love. Amen.

THERE ARE BEAR IN THE WOODS

In the Upper Peninsula of Michigan rifle season for deer hunting always begins on the 15th of November. Normally, this means that by the time deer hunters walk into the woods the Black Bear have already started to hibernate.

It is rare to see a bear in the woods during deer season. However, it is not impossible. In fact, there was one year when the weather was unusually warm for the middle of November and I was sitting in my deer blind, as usual, looking south at the power line opening when all of the sudden I saw something come out of the woods and I wasn't sure at first, what it was.

For a second I thought it was a big black dog. But then, I realized that it was a bear cub, and pretty soon another one running out of the woods and jumping around in the tall grass that covered the power line opening. I was amazed as I watched them run back and forth playing like two little children.

My feeling of amazement soon turned to a feeling of uncomfortableness when their mother came walking out into the power line. She was a big bear. I would guess that she weighed easily over 200 pounds and she was no more than 50 yards away from where I was sitting.

I watched her carefully as she stood protectively over her cubs for what seemed to be a long time. Eventually the mother bear and her two cubs scampered back into the woods and I took a deep breath.

It was only then that I realized I had my camera sitting on my lap. All the while I watching this mother bear and her two cubs playing in front of me I could have taken pictures of the whole thing.

I was so intent on watching what was happening, I never even thought once about my camera. Very often people do the opposite. They are so intent on taking pictures of what is going on in their lives and then uploading those pictures to "Facebook," or cataloging them on their computer that they never really have an opportunity to just experience the joy of the moment.

[1]Six days later, Jesus took with him Peter and James and his brother John and led them up a high mountain, by themselves.[2]And he was transfigured before them, and his face shone like the sun, and his clothes became dazzling white.[3]Suddenly there appeared to them Moses and Elijah, talking with him.[4]Then Peter said to Jesus, "Lord, it is good for us to be here; if you wish, I will make three dwellings here, one for you, one for Moses, and one for Elijah."[5]While he was still speaking, suddenly a bright cloud overshadowed them, and from the cloud a voice said, "This is my Son, the Beloved; with him I am well pleased; listen to him!"[6] (Matthew 17: 1-5)

Every day and every joy filled experience in life provides us with opportunities to celebrate the beauty of God's creation and the amazing grace and love of God that surrounds us. Instead of trying to capture each moment, as Peter wanted to do on the mount of transfiguration, God calls us to celebrate his presence as we continue our journey through life, treasuring the gifts of God in our hearts instead of cataloging them on a computer.

PRAYER: Ever present God, keep mindful of the wonders of creation that surround me each day. Let me be thankful those moments joy in my life that have provided a true sense of your wonder and love even as I am thankful for your presence in moments of struggle of doubt. Amen.

SURROUNDED BY TURKEYS

No doubt you've heard the expression, "It's hard to soar like an eagle when you are surrounded by turkeys." There are at least a couple of experiences that I have had while deer hunting that confirms the truth of such a statement.

On one occasion, I had walked out to a deer blind that was located on a ridge of hard woods in the middle of a swamp. I had arrived early in the morning so that it was still dark and I had carefully made as little noise as possible walking out to the blind in order to avoid alerting any deer of my presence. Quietly and anxiously I sat there waiting for the sun to come up and hoping to see some deer.

My attention was focused on the surroundings and my ears were pealed for any noise that might indicate the movement of a deer. The sun was just starting to show itself on the horizon when I heard a sound, it was kind of a "fluttering" sound and I wasn't sure exactly where it was coming from but it started to get louder and louder. I was on high alert, sensing that some kind of animal was approaching.

Suddenly the noise became startling loud as I began to see large creatures descending from the trees all around me. Before I knew what was happening, there must have been at least thirty turkeys on the ground that had been roosting in the trees that surrounded my blind. For a brief moment I thought it was an alien invasion! So there I sat, realizing that the turkeys had made so much noise there wasn't much chance of a deer coming anywhere near anytime soon.

On another occasion I was sitting in a blind that overlooked what used to be a corn field. The corn had been harvested and the field was right next to a swamp. It was a great place to hunt because deer would often come out of the swamp in order to eat the corn that was left lying on the ground.

Once again, I was quietly and anxiously waiting for any sign of deer movement when my eyes caught a glimpse of something else moving on the edge of the field. It was a turkey, and then there was another one and another one and another one until finally I counted 25 turkeys all walking out into the corn field and helping themselves to the corn that was left on the ground.

I watched them for quite a while and kept thinking to myself, "as long as those turkeys are in the field no deer are going to come and there will be less and less corn for the deer to eat."

So, finally I decided to do something about it. I decided to chase the turkeys away by firing a shot over their heads. I took aim over the middle of where the turkeys were feeding and let the shot go. Instantly those turkeys took off making all kinds of noise and flying in all kinds of different directions.

Some of them roosted in trees on the edge of the field and others landed on the ground somewhere in the swamp. I could still hear them cackling and making all kinds of noise in the woods for quite a while. And then, I saw another flock of turkeys coming from the other side of the field.

It was as if the first flock of turkeys had called for reinforcements because they were under attack. As soon as the second flock of turkeys started making their way into the field the firs flock of turkeys started to come out of hiding and went to join forces with the other flock which was now well into the field. At that point, I simply gave up and left my blind to go back to camp. Once again, "It's hard to soar like an eagle when you are surrounded by turkeys!"

There are times in life when you have to realize that you have little or no control over the circumstances and events that are taking place around you. As the "Serenity Prayer" suggests, it is at those times when you need to ask God to "Grant you the serenity to accept the things you cannot change; the courage to change the things you can; and the wisdom to know the difference."

[1][Jesus] was praying in a certain place, and after he had finished, one of his disciples said to him, "Lord, teach us to pray, as John taught his disciples."[2]He said to them, "When you pray, say:
Father, hallowed be your name.
Your kingdom come.
[3]Give us each day our daily bread.
[4]And forgive us our sins,
for we ourselves forgive everyone indebted to us.
And do not bring us to the time of trial." (Luke 11:1-4)

Instead of being frustrated when things don't go the way you want them to go, I have learned that it's best to be thankful for the daily bread that God provides for us without even asking.

Discerning the difference between needs and wants is an important exercise in humility that reminds me to keep my feet on the ground. Instead of always needing to "soar like an eagle," I should be thankful for the blessings of sight and sound that surround me every day, even when it happens to be the sight and sound of turkeys!

PRAYER; Patient and loving God, I am grateful that you never give up on me. When I complain and make noise because something is keeping me from getting what I want, open my eyes and my ears to see the gifts of your love that surround me each day. Remind me that I can be thankful and humbled by Your constant presence in my life. Amen.

REMEMBERING DEAR HUNTING FRIENDS

"For all the saints who from their labors rest, all who by faith before the world confessed, your name, O Jesus, be forever blest. Alleluia! Alleluia!"

I remember the first time I ever sang those words and at the same time felt their emotional impact as I connected the words together with the name of someone who had died. I was attending the funeral of my grandfather, my mother's father, and as we sang the words, "For all the saints who from their labors rest," I thought about my grandfather and how his life's work was all about confessing his faith and proclaiming the name of Jesus Christ.

I remember also, having a hard time singing those words because in that moment they were not just words, but they were words filled with both emotion and meaning. Since then, there have been many other occasions in which I have sung those words and felt their emotional impact as I have had to say good bye to more and more people in my life with whom I had developed a meaningful and emotional bond.

The older you get, the longer that list of people tends to be. When I first started hunting in the U.P. of Michigan I was only 30 years old. I was one of the "young guys" at camp. As the years have gone by, however, that has changed.

I am now one of the "old guys" at camp. And the number "older guys" that were there 30 years ago is getting fewer and fewer. Today, I remember all of them with deep appreciation and great respect.

Being a pastor, I have had the privilege of presiding over some of their funeral services and even a few graveside services in which their ashes were buried right next to their deer blinds.

It may sound strange to refer to a group of guys at deer camp as "saints," but I have come to know and believe that is what they are, not "perfect" by any means, but "saints" to be sure!

A professor that I had in seminary told us as young pastors going out into congregations for the first time that we should always be mindful of the fact that "wherever you go, you are standing on the shoulders of those who have gone before you!"

So it is at deer camp. There are many who have gone before me who have made it possible for me and for my son to celebrate a bond of friendship and genuinely caring relationships that bear witness to the name of Jesus and His unconditional love for us all.

Today, when I sing the words, "For all the saints who from their labors rest…." I now think of my grandfather, John and I also think of Elmer, Elsie, Ken, Sonny, Walter, Harold, Marlin, Tom, and Chuck.

The list keeps growing as the years go by but I can still manage to get the words out because my faith is not shaken by their death, but is rather strengthened by the witness of their lives.

Someone once asked me if I thought there would be deer hunting in heaven and I responded by saying that I believe heaven is a place that is so wonderful that no one is going to be disappointed when they close their eyes in death and then open them in heaven.

Therefore if I choose to believe that there will be deer hunting in heaven, well that's OK. It is certainly one way of picturing what a perfect life might look like.

Either way, I am looking forward to seeing all my "Dear Hunting Friends" again. Until then, I continue to do my best to honor their memory by living my life bearing witness to the name of Jesus and His unconditional love for all people.

PRAYER: *Oh, blest communion, fellowship divine,*

we feebly struggle, they in glory shine;

yet all are one within your great design.

Alleluia! Alleluia! Amen.

DRINKING COFFEE IN A TREE STAND

My method of deer hunting is based upon the idea that if you sit in one spot long enough you will get a chance to shoot a deer. Therefore, I have a deer blind that is designed to stay in one spot.

Not everyone agrees with this method of deer hunting. One of the guys in our camp, in particular, believes that you need to have options when it comes to deer blinds.

Over the years he has probably built at least 2 or 3 deer blinds in different locations and has also set up at least 2 or 3 tree stands in different locations.

Every morning during the deer season he has to make a decision about where he will be sitting that morning. The problem with having so many choices, of course, is that no matter what choice you make you run the risk of a big buck showing up at one of the other locations.

On this particular morning he had made his decision about where he was going to sit but then he opened up the opportunity for me to choose one of the other locations, if I so desired. I had not been seeing any deer in the one deer blind where I had been sitting for the previous 3 days, so I was interested in trying a new place.

"This is a new tree stand that I just put up this year," he said, "and there are a lot of trails that go right passed where you would be sitting." So, the decision was made. I headed out that morning for a tree stand that I had never seen before. He had given me pretty specific directions and so I found the tree stand with no problems.

I had a back pack with my supplies for the morning and my rifle, which I tied to a rope and then climbed the ladder to get into the tree stand before pulling the rifle up with the rope. It took just a little bit of time for me to get situated. I loaded my rifle and hang my backpack from the tree stand and then, I began to wait watch.

I suppose it was about an hour before I started to wonder if this was a good idea. Nothing was happening in this location either. So, I decided to pour myself a cup of coffee. I had a thermos of coffee in my backpack and I laid my rifle over my lap while I opened the backpack up, took out the thermos and poured myself a hot cup of coffee.

It was a brisk morning and so the hot coffee tasted pretty good only now I began to realize that if a deer came out, I would have no place to put my coffee cup so that I could pick up my rifle.

No sooner did I have that thought when a deer came prancing out into a clearing in front of me. It was a doe and she began to sniff the air. Evidently she could smell the coffee. Now here came another deer and it was a spike horn buck and he wasn't interested in smelling any except that doe!

And so began a back and forth dance between the doe and the buck taking place right in front of me. The buck would run up towards the doe and the doe would snort and run somewhere else. The buck was undeterred and would continue to chase after the doe and around and around they went.

There I sat watching this whole thing take place and there was nothing else I could do, except just watch. I couldn't even drink the coffee in my cup because I was afraid my movement would chase them away. Finally, they did wander off in different directions. By that time, my coffee was cold and I had learned another important lesson, "when hunting in someone else's blind make sure you know in advance whether it has a cup holder or not!"

"Then Jesus called the twelve together and gave them power and authority over all demons and to cure diseases, and he sent them out to proclaim the kingdom of God and to heal. He said to them, "Take nothing for your journey, no staff, nor bag, nor bread, nor money — not even an extra tunic." (Luke 9:1-3)

There are times in our lives when we burden ourselves with so many extra things that we are no longer to accomplish that which is most important. The world is filled with distractions and desires and we are often weak and easily distracted.

PRAYER: God I thank you that you are never so distracted that you are not be able to hear my prayers and direct my ways. I am also grateful for the fullness of your grace that forgives me for my own distractions which often keep me from doing your will. Continue to guide me and teach me according to Your will even as you continue to call me to be faithful to Your word. Amen.

"BONNIE'S BUNS" AND OTHER DEER CAMP DELICASIES

One thing you can be sure of when you spend time at deer camp is that you will probably not be losing any weight. The kind of food that is served at deer camp is usually high in calories, cholesterol and saturated fats.

A typical menu for any given day might include fried eggs, bacon, sausage, pancakes, cheese and, of course, venison, served in a variety of ways.

We might have venison sausage, venison steak, venison chili, venison burgers, venison roast or any combination of the above. Along with the venison there will also be a variety of side dishes including potatoes, beans, onions, sauerkraut and of course, bread and butter!

Ever since I can remember going to deer camp included being able to enjoy "Bonnie's buns." Every year, one of the couples who hunt with our group has provided a supply of homemade buns, enough for the whole crew to eat for the entire season. Since the wife who makes those buns is named "Bonnie," they have affectionately been referred to as "Bonnie's Buns."

"Go to the pantry and get a bag of Bonnie's buns," someone might say. Or, "Does anyone know if we have anymore of Bonnie's buns left?" Or, "someone needs to call Bonnie and tell her we need more of her buns!" These are the kind of tongue in cheek innuendos that make deer camp unique. And, of course, they are always received by "Bonnie" as a compliment.

There is no doubt that "Bonnie" is highly respected and greatly appreciated by everyone at camp. If there were any indication that she took offense to the reference of "Bonnie's buns" that phrase would never ever be heard again. It's not always what you say at camp that matters as much as it is what you mean and what is being heard that matters most of all.

St. Paul says, *"Though I am free with respect to all, I have made myself a slave to all, so that I might win more of them.[20] To the Jews I became as a Jew, in order to win Jews. To those under the law I became as one under the law (though I myself am not under the law) so that I might win those under the law.*

[21]To those outside the law I became as one outside the law (though I am not free from God's law but am under Christ's law) so that I might win those outside the law.[22]To the weak I became weak, so that I might win the weak. I have become all things to all people, that I might by all means save some.[23]I do it all for the sake of the gospel, so that I may share in its blessings." (1 Corinthians 9:19-23)

What makes deer camp such an enjoyable experience is the fact that the food and the conversations that we share together are reflections of a bond of friendship and respect that exists between those who gather there. There is a sense of freedom then within that bond of friendship that allows everyone to share in the blessings of the gospel within the context of deer camp. How great is that!

PRAYER: Great and loving God, keep me always mindful of how my words are being received by others so that I might never speak in such a way that offends but always speak words that honor and respect the other even as I give thanks for the relationship that we share together as brothers and sisters in Christ. Amen.

LEAVING THE BLIND TOO EARLY

Typically during deer season I will the camp around 6:00 am, just before the sun if rising, in order to get to my blind around 6:20 am. This gives me time to get situated and ready so that when the sun does come up I am prepared for whatever happens. I will sit in my blind until about 9:30 am, and then I will start getting ready to go back to camp for breakfast.

That is my normal routine. Sometimes, if the weather is warm enough, I will sit longer and sometimes, if the weather is cold, I will sit for a shorter period of time. How long I sit is also somewhat dependent upon whether or not I have been seeing any deer.

If I have been seeing deer I will probably sit longer. If I am not seeing any deer, I will probably go back to camp sooner. On one particular day a few years ago it was cold and I wasn't seeing any deer at all. So, when it got to be around 9:00 am I was getting tired of sitting and decided to get up and go back to camp for some breakfast.

As I climbed out of the blind I decided that before heading back to the camp I would take a walk down to the edge of the power line opening, which was about 75 yards south of my blind so that I could take a look at a scraping that one of the other hunters at camp had told me that he saw before the season started.

I walked to the edge of the power line opening and began to look into the woods to locate the scrape. Sure enough, there it was, just about 15 feet into the woods, a fresh scrape. "Ok," I thought, "there must be a buck working this area."

I turned around to head back to camp and when I looked up at my blind, 75 yards away, there was a buck standing right next to my blind! I froze right where I was standing and looked at that buck who was staring directly at me.

It had antlers that were outside of its ears and pretty high, I would guess it to be at least an 8 point buck. We stared at each other for a few seconds and then I slowly tried to raise my rifle, but as soon as I made a move, that buck just took off into the woods behind my blind.

"There it was, gone!"

This kind of thing doesn't just happen at deer camp. There are a lot of times in life when because of a poor decision we make or a bad choice or because of any number of other random circumstances at work affecting our behavior, the one thing that we are seeking, the one thing that we have set out to achieve is suddenly no longer achievable.

"There it is, gone!"

Still, there are worse things than missing out on getting a nice buck during hunting season. The one thing that should be most important to us and be the focus of our concentration on any given day is, of course, the Kingdom of God.

"Therefore do not worry, saying, 'What will we eat?' or 'What will we drink?' or 'What will we wear? For it is the Gentiles who strive for all these things; and indeed your heavenly Father knows that you need all these things. But strive first for the kingdom of God and his righteousness, and all these things will be given to you as well." (Matthew 6:31-33)

Unfortunately, we very often let the Kingdom of God slip right through our hands. We miss out on opportunities to bear witness to the love and light of Jesus Christ because, instead, we are too busy worrying about ourselves.

The good news is that God believes in giving us second chances and even third and fourth and fifth chances. His love for us is unconditional and His forgiveness is unbounded. At the same time, God also wants us to learn from our mistakes.

PRAYER: God of grace and mercy and unbounded patience we thank you for giving us so many second chances as we seek to put your Kingdom's priorities before our own. Help us to learn patience as we seek out opportunities to serve You by loving others in your name. Amen.

AN EIGHT POINT SPIKE

As I have mentioned earlier, several years ago we initiated the practice of "Quality Deer Management" at deer camp, which means that everyone agrees to not shoot a buck that has less than 3 point on one side of his antlers and no does, unless the camp master says we need meat for the camp.

I wasn't sure about this new way of hunting but I was willing to give it a chance. However, on one particular year, following the adoption of "QDM," I found myself seeing all kinds of does and bucks but none of the bucks met the standards that we had set. I would come back from hunting and describe how I saw several does; two spike horn bucks and one fork horn but, "nothing that I could shoot!"

This went on for the first three days of hunting until finally, on the evening before my last morning hunt, the camp master said to me, "Roland, if you see a spike horn buck tomorrow morning go ahead and shoot it, I don't want you go home empty handed." "Really," I said, "thanks, I'll have to give that some thought!"

So the next morning I got to my blind early, fully expecting to see the same parade of deer walking by that I had been seeing for the previous three days. Only now, guess what? There was nothing. There were no does and certainly no bucks anywhere in sight. I remember thinking to myself, "sure, this is my luck as soon as I have permission to shoot a spike horn buck they all disappear."

I was pretty disappointed sitting there that morning, fully expecting that I would end up going home without anything when, just about the time when I was getting ready to pack things up and go back to camp I saw something move in the tall grass at the edge of the power line opening. I raised my scope to take a look and sure enough, there was a deer standing there.

I could only see the very top of his back and his dead was down so I didn't know at first if it was a doe or a spike horn buck. And then it lifted its head and I realized it was neither. It was a very nice eight point buck just standing there.

With its head raised he gave me an opportunity to take a neck shot and down he went. I could hardly believe my eyes. Here I was feeling all disappointed and sorry for myself because the does and spike horn bucks I had been seeing earlier had all disappeared, but the reason they were gone was because this eight point buck, the dominate buck, had come back into the area.

When I got back to camp I thought I would have a little fun with the camp master. "Well, did you get anything this morning," he asked. And I responded, "Yes I did." "Good," he said, "what did you get?" Keeping as straight of a face as possible, I responded, "a spike horn buck."

I could tell that he was just a little disappointed but he managed to congratulate me anyway and he said, "Well that's good, I'm glad you have something to take home with you. How big are the spikes?" "Pretty big," I said, "I guess you could call it an eight point spike!"

"What?" he replied, "You've got to be kidding me?" No, I wasn't kidding about the eight point buck that I had just shot and I was even now a more firm believer the practice of Quality Deer Management.

Sometimes when things change we have a hard time dealing with those changes and we might even be resentful of the fact that things don't just stay the same way they have always been. But not all changes are bad. Many changes, in fact, are actually really good.

"A lawyer asked [Jesus] a question to test him. Teacher, which commandment in the law is the greatest? He said to him," 'You shall love the Lord your God with all your heart, and with all your soul, and with all your mind.' This is the greatest and first commandment. And a second is like it: 'You shall love your neighbor as yourself.' On these two commandments hang all the law and the prophets." (Matthew 22:35-40)

For years, the Jews had depended upon the 10 commandments and the laws and rules that had been written about those commandments to be that which would guide the way they lived and the way they interacted with other people. And then Jesus came along and suggested that the heart of those commandments is summed up in just one commandment, the commandment to love; both God and neighbor.

Not everyone was happy with this change that Jesus was introducing, but the truth is, love is the only thing that can solve the problems of the world in which we live and at the same time fill our lives with joy. Give it a chance and see what happens.

DEER CAMP DEVOTIONS

PRAYER: Heavenly Father, we are eternally grateful for the law of love that you have introduced to us through the life, death and resurrection of Jesus Christ. Help us to be open to the newness of loving others even as you have loved us. Keep us from being rigid or resentful in relationship to other people and fill us with the joy that comes only from the unconditional love that you daily pour out upon us. Amen.

HOW DARK IS THE SWAMP?

When I head up north to go deer hunting as soon as I cross over into Michigan I always stop to buy my deer hunting license. Because I hunt with two different hunting camps it has been my practice to purchase what is called a "combo" hunting license.

This hunting license allows me to shoot two bucks. I buy this license, not because I expect to shoot two bucks, but only because, if I do shoot a buck in the first camp where I am hunting I want to be able to still legally hunt when I go over to the second deer hunting camp.

There have been a "few" times when I have been fortunate enough to get two bucks but that typically a rare occasion. This past year I was successful in shooting a buck while hunting at the first camp and so I was able to bring my buck over to the second camp and hang it on their buck pole and celebrate my good fortune with them.

When it was time to go hunting then at the second camp, since I already had a buck hanging on the pole, the pressure was off. "Where do you want me to sit," I asked, and the camp master of this second camp told me, "well, since you already have a buck, and my son had to go home, why don't you go sit behind the farm in his blind."

He then proceeded to tell me that his son had been sitting in that blind for the previous four days without seeing any deer. "That's alright with me," I responded and off I went to take my place in his son's blind. I was happy because this blind was insulated and had a heater inside of it. It was very comfortable.

I was just enjoying the scenery, watching the sun set and thinking about how lucky I was to already have a buck and to be able to share the hunting camp experience with good friends. And then, I saw something move on the other side of the field that I was watching. The blind I was sitting in was on the edge of a forty acre field and because the sun was setting directly in front of me I wasn't quite sure what I was looking at so I raised my rifle and looked through the scope.

There it was, a buck was standing on the other side of the field and from 200 yards away I could tell that he had a big rack. My heart started pounding as I waited for him to move closer.

Instead of moving closer, however, this buck started to move to the south west away from where I was sitting. If I wanted to get a shot I had to take it before it got too far away and so I shot. The buck started running and as it was running I fired off three more shots before I saw the buck disappear into the swamp on the other side of the field.

I sat there for a few minutes trying to regain my composure and making mental note of exactly where it was that I saw that buck go into the swamp. My cell phone buzzed, it was the camp master wanting to know if the shots he heard were mine. "Yes," I responded. "Was it a buck," he asked. "Yes," I said, "a big one." "Did you get it," he asked. "I don't know," I responded, I hope so."

He then sent me a text saying that he would come over to help me look as soon as he could. In the meantime, I began walking across the field towards the spot that I had marked where I thought the buck left the field and went into the swamp.

There was snow on the ground and when I got to the other side of the field it didn't take me long to find a blood trail leading into the swamp. By the time my friend, the camp master, arrived it was already dark and I showed him the blood trail that I had found.

With flashlights in hand we both entered into the swamp following the blood trail. Because it had been a cold season the swamp was frozen over and the snow on the ground made the blood trail pretty easy to follow, except for the fact that this buck was weaving back and forth between, over and under some pretty thick brush.

We slowly but steadily followed his trail until finally we found him. It was a really nice eight point buck. In that moment, I was excited and grateful. My friend congratulated me and then said, "You are the luckiest hunter I've ever known!" I began the process of field dressing the deer as my friend held the flash light so that I could see what I was doing and when it was all done I was surprised to hear my friend say, "I'm not really sure where we are right now and my cell phone just died. We'd better turn off our flashlights for a while to save batteries while we try and figure out which way to go."

I gave him my cell phone so that he could call one of his other sons and have him drive out to the swamp where we were. "When you get here," he told him, "beep your horn so we can direct you to where we are." And then we turned off our flash lights and waited.

I never knew how dark a swamp could be until that moment. It was so dark you couldn't even see your own hand in front of your face. At that moment my friend said, "I'm a little worried because we have all this blood around us and there are wolves in this swamp."

When talking to his disciples just before they were leaving on a mission trip, Jesus said, *"See, I am sending you out like sheep into the midst of wolves; so be wise as serpents and innocent as doves." (Matthew 10:16)* It is a dangerous and dark world that we live in filled with all kinds of predators. St. Paul, however, understood that the predators of this world are not flesh and blood.

"Be strong in the Lord," he says, *"and in the strength of his power. Put on the whole armor of God, so that you may be able to stand against the wiles of the devil. For our struggle is not against enemies of blood and flesh, but against the rulers, against the authorities, against the cosmic powers of this present darkness, against the spiritual forces of evil in the heavenly places." (Ephesians 6:1—12)*

The armor of God, of course, that Paul is talking about has nothing to do with weapons or shields, but rather with the Word of God made visible in the loving actions that we share with all people. Whenever we proclaim God's love by actually loving the way that God loves us then we allow the light of His love to shine in the darkness of the world.

It didn't take long before my friend's son showed up and we hear him beep his horn. We turned our flashlights on and he could see where we were. He brought a couple of his friends with and they came out to where we were and dragged my buck out of the swamp.

We stopped before loading the buck into the truck in order to take a picture in the light of God's love that surrounded us and filled the moment with joy and there were smiles all around!

PRAYER: God of light and love. Fill us daily with the joy of your unconditional love and give us courage to face the darkness of this world knowing that there is no darkness that can overcome your light which is ours forever in Christ Jesus. Amen.

WHAT HAPPENS AT CAMP STAYS AT CAMP!

There are many stories that could be told about things that have happened at deer camp, but there is also a universally accepted rule that suggests, "What happens at camp stays at camp!" That is to say, deer camp is supposed to be a place where a person can relax and enjoy them self without having to worry about saying or doing something that might end up turning into an embarrassing story that they later have to try and explain or apologize for.

Although it may be true that there are some stories from deer camp which are best left untold, it is also true that most of the stories from deer camp are stories that deserve to be told simply because they are stories that reflect the true nature and character of those who gather together every year, not just to hunt deer, but also to encourage and support each other and to sustain and nurture the enduring friendships that have formed over the years.

For me, going to deer camp has always been a kind of temporary escape from the realities and challenges of parish ministry. It is a place where I can go and not have to worry about "being a pastor." Instead, I can just be one of the "guys." But the truth is, I am a pastor and the people that I hunt with at deer camp are also people of faith.

I remember one night showing up at deer camp and a few of the guys were sitting around the kitchen table playing cards. As soon as I walked in the door and before I had a chance to even carry my sleeping bag into the bunk room, one of the guys said, "hey, preacher, you're just the guy we need to answer a question for us. We were just talking about how in the bible it sometimes refers to the twelve disciples and the twelve apostles. So maybe you can tell us, what's the difference between being a disciple and being an apostle?" "Really," I responded, "that's what you were talking about?" "Yes," they said, "so, what's the difference?"

I went on to explain that disciples are like students who are learning from a teacher and that apostles are like students who have graduated and who are being sent out into the world in order to apply what they have learned in a meaningful way.

As I now reflect on that "deer camp conversation," I realize that I have been both disciple and apostle in relationship to my friends at deer camp and that God has been patiently and persistently guiding me along the way.

At the end of the Gospel of John, the author writes, *"Now Jesus did many other signs in the presence of the disciples which are not written in this book, but these are written so that you may believe that Jesus is the Christ, the Son of God, and that by believing, you may have life in His name."(John 20:30, 31)*

Even so, I would say, there are many other stories that could be told about the things that have happened at deer camp which are not written in this book, but these stories have been written so that you may believe that Jesus is the Christ, the Son of God and that God is also patiently and persistently guiding you to be both disciple and apostle. Yes, even at deer camp!

PRAYER: Loving God, I thank you for the opportunities that I have every day to be both disciple and apostle in your Kingdom. Continue to teach me what I need to know about your love through the relationships that I share with others and continue also to challenge me to teach others as I am sent into the world to be a living example of your love in their lives. Amen.

ABOUT THE AUTHOR

Roland Lindeman is an ordained minister in the Evangelical Lutheran Church in America. He is currently retired and living in Oshkosh, Wisconsin after having served parishes for over 39 years. Roland started deer hunting in 1979 when he was serving his first parish in Eveleth, Minnesota. A love for deer hunting continued to grow as he developed deer hunting relationships with members of his second parish in Wallace, Michigan. Roland is married to his wife, Bonnie and together they have two children, Anthony and Amy.

Made in the USA
Lexington, KY
27 June 2019